VINCENT RYAN

LENT AND
HOLY WEEK

VERITAS PUBLICATIONS
FOWLER WRIGHT BOOKS LTD

First edition published 1976
This edition first published 1983 by
Veritas Publications
7/8 Lower Abbey Street
Dublin 1
and
Fowler Wright Books Ltd
Leominster, Herefordshire

ISBN: 0 86217 086 9
Cover designed by Steven Hope
Typeset by Printset and Design Ltd
Printed in the Republic of Ireland by
Mount Salus Press

Contents

PREFACE

This work does not differ substantially from the first edition which appeared in 1976. But it does contain some new material which I shall briefly describe. In the first place, I have re-written the first chapter to present the season of Lent in a more dynamic way as the *Journey to Easter,* a pilgrimage of faith and conversion and a microcosm of life itself. Then, in the following two chapters, which treat of Lent as a baptismal and a penitential time, I have taken account of the experience gained in recent years of the restored catechumenate, adult baptism and communal celebrations of penance.

There is one new chapter, *Sunday Preaching during Lent.* This is intended as a guide to priests who would like to plan a course of homilies corresponding to the three-year cycle of readings. The lectionary does in fact enable us to select a particular theme for the Sundays of each year. It is good to vary our approach and to exploit to the full the riches of the Lenten readings.

There has been little alteration in the section on Holy Week. Here I have simply re-arranged the material to bring out more clearly the distinctive features and time-limits of each day of the sacred triduum. It is now more evident that this period begins with the evening Mass on Holy Thursday. Also our commentary on the Easter Vigil is now incorporated within the chapter on Easter Sunday, emphasising the fact that the Vigil Mass is indeed that of the Sunday and of the Resurrection.

Finally, a new Bibliography has been prepared. This includes books and articles on Lent and Holy Week which have appeared in recent years. They are in English and are reasonably accessible.

I wish to thank Mr Seán O Boyle, Director of Veritas Publications, for having invited me to prepare this new edition, and also Fr Brian Magee, liturgical editor, for his advice and assistance.

Vincent Ryan, OSB
First Sunday of Advent, 1982

1

THE JOURNEY TO EASTER

Life is a journey, a pilgrimage. We are a people on the move, bound for our homeland in heaven. We have not here a lasting city, pilgrims and exiles that we are. Such is the message of scripture, especially of the New Testament. It is a message which in practice we tend to ignore or prefer not to think about. It is the world of the here-and-now that absorbs our attention. It is as though nothing lay beyond the world of the visible and material. We lose our sense of direction and of purpose, we forget that a higher destiny awaits us.

From time to time the journey must be resumed with fresh impetus. Lent is such a time, a "favourable time", when we set out with new purpose on the journey which leads ultimately to God. Our immediate objective is Easter, the Christian Passover, but this is itself a symbol and foretaste of the paschal feast of heaven. Thus the Lenten season may be viewed as a microcosm of life itself.

The concept of a journey fits in very well with the Church's understanding of Lent. The forty days correspond not only with the time Jesus spent in the desert but also with the forty years the children of Israel spent in journeying to the Promised Land. Lent is a kind of résumé of this great period of salvation history. The daily Old Testament readings for the office lead us stage by stage from the exodus from Egypt to the arrival at the fair land promised to Moses and his people. We too are being called out of Egypt, from the tyranny of sin and enslavement to passions, to the freedom of God's children.

The liturgies of the Christian East also represent Lent as a journey. At the beginning of this penitential time the faithful of the Greek Orthodox church are alerted by this pressing

9

invitation: "Let us set out with joy upon the season of the fast." The journey is to be undertaken in a spirit of joy. Not that the journey itself will be enjoyable or easy but because we look towards the goal with eager longing. Lent is the way to Easter, to rejoicing, to life renewed.

Our joy is the joy of expectancy, of eager preparation. This joyful mood is well evoked in the first of the prefaces for Lent: "Each year you give us this joyful season when we prepare to celebrate the paschal mystery with mind and heart renewed." The translation misses a nuance in the Latin original which places the accent on anticipation rather than on present possession. It would be better rendered, "to look forward with joy (*in gaudio expectare*) to the Easter festival". St Benedict in his *Rule for Monks* uses a similar phrase, encouraging his monks during the season of Lent to "look forward to holy Easter with the joy of spiritual longing".[1]

The way to this joy is through the narrow gate of penance. It would be an illusion to expect an effortless or an instant joy. What is involved is a discipline which may go very much against the grain. There will be an element of combat, of self-restraint, of sticking-it-out. On Ash Wednesday, in the opening prayer of the Mass, we ask the Lord to "protect us in our struggle against evil as we begin the discipline of Lent". So we must brace ourselves for battle. But there must be no pharisaical putting on of long faces. The offering must be joyfully made, since "God loves a cheerful giver" (2 *Cor* 9: 7). In the spirit of the Oriental liturgy let us exclaim: "There are forty days in the fast; let us keep them all with joy."[2]

Lent is a journey of faith and conversion. It is the acceptance of Christ's call to take up our cross and follow him. He is the Way and we must follow in that way. Scripture allows us no delay: "Let us run with perseverance the race that is set before us, looking to Jesus, the pioneer and perfecter of our faith" (*Heb* 12: 2 RSV). Our journey, as Lent progresses, focuses more and more on the final journey of Jesus to Jerusalem, to Calvary and on to glory. And it is our prayer that we may accompany him all the way. This is expressed in one of the petitions of the morning office: "You went up to Jerusalem to endure the Passion and

10

enter into your glory; lead your Church into the paschal feast of eternal life'' (Friday 2 and 4 of Lent).

As a time of penance Lent can be thought of as a *return journey*. It represents the return of man to Paradise from which he had been banished by his rebellion. The entry is no longer barred: it has been re-opened by the Cross of Christ. In the words of St Benedict: ''Receive willingly and carry out effectively your loving father's advice, that by the labour of obedience you may return to him from whom you had departed by the sloth of disobedience.''[3]

The return journey of Lent is perhaps best represented by the parable of the ''prodigal son'' (*Lk* 15: 11-32) which is read on Saturday of the second week and on the fourth Sunday of Year C. This foolish younger son, who goes his own way and squanders his patrimony, represents not only the great sinner who does penance, but, in some sense, all of us. Who has not strayed from the Father's house? Which one of us has not squandered God's gifts! And so we can identify with this prodigal son and at the beginning of the penitential season take the first resolute step that he took: ''I will leave this place and go to my Father.''

A programme for Lent. Lent is no longer the rigorous time it used to be. For one thing, the fast has been greatly mitigated. During this period life goes on much the same as at other times of the year. There is the ceremony of receiving ashes on our foreheads at the beginning of Lent, and we may make a good resolution to undertake this or do without that. One could not claim that this amounts to very much in the way of generosity or self-sacrifice.

True, Lent is not a very demanding time if we consider it simply in terms of external observances. These the Church no longer wishes to spell out for us, or *weigh out* for us if it is a question of fasting. Much is left to our own individual judgement and spirit of generosity. The penitential practices we may adopt are but the tokens of what should be an attitude of mind and heart. It is for each one to try to determine what is God's will for him or her. It is for each one in prayer to ask, ''Lord, what would you have me do?'' And since life has its own built-in penances, it

11

may be the best penance of all to accept these patiently and generously.

Lent is no mere formality. It has not lost its relevance or its challenge. Indeed in some ways it is more demanding than in the past. It is not an easy thing to accept the call to conversion of heart, to penance and renewal; and this call is made insistently during Lent. The challenge to judge our lives by the demands of the Gospel is not lightly accepted. The Lenten liturgy presents us with just such a challenge, requiring of us to take our lives seriously in hand.

It would be a mistake, however, to regard the effort as ours and ours alone. This is not so, since it is really God who in this season of grace takes the Church in hand, purifying and renewing it. As the second Lenten preface so well puts it: "This great season of grace is your gift to your family to renew us in spirit." And so we should welcome it as a gift from God. An attitude of humble and grateful acceptance is recommended to our fellow-Christians of the Orthodox Church in these words heard at the beginning of Lent: "Come, O ye people, and today let us accept the grace of the fast as a gift from God."[4]

The grace of Easter is already operative during Lent, strengthening and renewing the Church. The paschal mystery is at work in those preparing for baptism and in those renewing their baptismal dedication. The risen Lord is drawing all men to himself. The Good Shepherd is searching for the lost sheep and bringing them home.

Lent is a time of renewal. The Old English word *lencten*, from which our "Lent" derives, simply meant the season of spring, the time of year when the days lengthen and all nature comes alive after the sleep of winter. The penitential time coincides with the season of spring. Or so it does in countries of the northern hemisphere. Different circumstances obtain in other parts of the world, say in Africa or Australia. (And even in Britain and Ireland due allowance must be made for the vagaries of our weather!)

Let us then respond to this symbolism of nature, and see reflected in the trees, shrubs and flowers what is happening in the world of grace. It is the one Creator who is at work in the order of

12

nature and in that of grace; and so we can truly exclaim at the beginning of this season: "The springtime of the fast has dawned, the flower of repentance has begun to open."[5]

A recurrent theme in the prayers of the missal during Lent is that of renewal.[6] This renewal is attributed not to our ascetic efforts but to God's mercy. It is he who takes the initiative and sees the work through. He makes use of the fast and the penance, prayer and sacraments to purify and renew the Church. As members of that Church we must dispose ourselves to receive his gift, and we must pray earnestly: "Renew us, Lord, in your Spirit" (petition from Morning Prayer, Wednesday of fifth week).

Lent is then a spring-time, a period of renewal and growth in the life of the Spirit. And this renewal, which should reach its climax at Easter, will continue in the post-paschal season in the weeks leading up to Pentecost. And here I would like to conclude this reflection on the relationship of Lent and spring by quoting a sixth-century Latin hymn beautifully translated by Fr Ronald Knox:

> The day is come, the accepted day,
> when grace, like nature, flowers anew;
> Trained by thy hand, the surer way,
> Rejoice we in our spring-time too.[7]

NOTES

1. *The Rule of St Benedict,* Ch. 49, "On the Observance of Lent". See J. McCann's edition, Sheed & Ward, London, 1976.
2. See *The Lenten Tridion,* translated by Mother Mary and Archimandrite Kallistos Ware, Faber & Faber, London & Boston, p. 23.
3. From the Prologue to the Rule.
4. *The Lenten Tridion,* p. 23.
5. On same page as above.
6. See for example the opening prayer for Monday of 4th week: "Father, creator, you give the world new life by your sacraments. May we, your Church, grow in your life and continue to receive your help on earth." The theme is also found in the prayers over the offerings and in the prayers after communion.
7. See Vol. 2 of *The Divine Office,* Appendix, p. 571.

2

LENT AS PREPARATION FOR BAPTISM

Joining the catechumens. Lent may be likened to a retreat or mission for the whole Church. One of the climaxes of a parish retreat is the renewal of baptismal promises by the whole congregation. One of the great climactic moments of the Easter liturgy is the same solemn ceremony of renewal in the course of the paschal vigil; during the weeks of Lent the Church is preparing us for that moment.

Traditionally, Easter is the most appropriate time for the conferring of baptism; the weeks of Lent represent the time of immediate preparation for this event. In the fifth and sixth centuries adult baptism was still the norm in Rome, and in the weeks immediately preceding Easter, the catechumens underwent a fairly intense preparation. This consisted of frequent meetings for prayers and instruction, blessings and exorcisms, as well as the learning of certain prayers.

It is good for us to recall what a difficult and even hazardous undertaking baptism was in the early centuries. It was a serious commitment exposing the candidate to the mistrust, ridicule or open persecution of the pagan society around him. It was not lightly undertaken, and the Church hesitated to confer baptism on those who gave little evidence of being serious in their intentions.

To be baptised meant, both literally and metaphorically, to take the plunge; literally, because baptism was by immersion; metaphorically, because it implied a once-for-all commitment and the adoption of a whole new way of life.

For the majority of Christians, baptised in infancy, no such commitment was involved. It is vitally important, however, that we do not remain Christians in name only, but that each

15

one of us ratifies his or her baptism at an age when this becomes possible. One such occasion is confirmation when the child renews the promises made on his behalf at baptism. There will be many other occasions throughout adult life; baptism is, after all, a permanent sacrament.

During Lent we prepare to renew our baptismal obligations at Easter. The Church invites us to join the ranks of the adult catechumens. In their company we can learn what it means to be a Christian. We follow them in their pilgrimage of faith.

The catechumenate revived. The ancient liturgy of the catechumenate has in our own times been revived, not only in the so-called mission countries but also in Europe, America and other parts of the world. In France organised catechumenal centres were in operation some years before the Second Vatican Council.[1] Of decisive importance was the promulgation of the rite for the Christian initiation of adults on 6 January 1972.[2] In the opinion of prominent liturgists, such as Fr Aidan Kavanagh, OSB, this must be considered one of the most outstanding liturgical reforms to emanate from Vatican II.[3]

It is clear from an examination of this *ordo* that the Church recognises the need for preparatory stages leading up to baptism, each of these stages being sanctified by appropriate rites. The final stage of this process is situated within the liturgical framework of Lent and Holy Week. Let us briefly describe what takes place.

On the first Sunday of Lent the catechumens are formally inscribed for baptism. This takes place in a little ceremony included within the Mass rite. The Church has now accepted them as candidates for the sacraments of Christian initiation. On the third, fourth and fifth Sundays of Lent, these candidates (*electi,* chosen ones, to use the ancient title) are again assembled in church to hear the word of God and receive the Church's blessing. As we shall see, the whole Liturgy of the Word for these Sundays is aimed at their instruction.

Also during Lent the ceremony of the "traditions" takes place. That is the solemn "tradition" or handing over to the catechumens of the two most precious formulas in Christian faith and piety: the Apostles' Creed and the Lord's Prayer.

16

They are entrusted with these prayers which they are to learn and treasure. Finally, at the high-point of the Church's year, within the celebration of the Easter Vigil, these "chosen ones" complete their initiation by the reception of baptism and first communion.

This initiation in stages corresponds to the catechumen's progress in faith. It is intended to consolidate that faith. There can be no doubt that it is the Church's intention to establish very clearly the link between faith and baptism; and the kind of faith she wishes to elicit is not just intellectual assent to a corpus of doctrines, but a *living* faith implying conversion of heart and commitment to Jesus Christ.

The candidate for baptism may well feel daunted by the demands made on him or her in becoming a Christian. This was so in the early Church, and so it is again in this present era. But here is where the Church exercises her maternal role. She supports the catechumens by her prayer and solicitude. All the faithful, especially during the weeks of Lent, are exhorted to pray for these candidates for baptism that they may persevere in their resolve in spite of temptations and difficulties. If this is the duty of the whole Church, it is especially incumbent on the local Christian community, the parish, to pray for, to support, and to welcome these prospective new members.

Although a decade has elapsed since the promulgation of the new rite of the Christian initiation of adults, it has to be admitted that neither its full significance nor rich potential have been realised. Where it has been implemented the results are very encouraging. Pastors speak of the beneficial effects of a restored catechumenate in their parishes. Fr Raymond Kemp, pastor of a parish in Washington, DC, and author of *A Journey in Faith*, claims that the new rite of adult initiation has effected quite a transformation in the parish community. He declares: "Without question, the restoration of the catechumenate has restored our parish and has been the prime force in helping us realise that we exist to initiate adults into the saving death-resurrection of Christ."[4]

We may well envy the parish which has catechumens and

where the new rite has been implemented. The courage and resolve of these adult men and women publicly professing their faith and submitting to the rites of the Church, cannot fail to challenge our own faith. We are reminded of the necessity for all Christians to be continually converted to Christ. We are obliged to reconsider and renew our own faith and commitment. As a result of all this, the faith of the whole community is enriched.

In a country like Ireland, where an overwhelming percentage of the population are baptised Christians, the question of a catechumenate and adult baptism may not seem to have much pastoral importance. But here, too, the theology and pastoral emphasis of the new rite need to be studied. Such a study will lead us to a deeper understanding of the Church and of the role of faith in the Christian life. It may also suggest a pastoral strategy for dealing with the Catholic-Christians whose faith is superficial, the "baptised catechumens" in our midst.

The baptismal readings. We have referred to the third, fourth and fifth Sundays of Lent as being of special significance for the catechumens. The readings were chosen to throw light on the mystery of baptism. In the new Roman lectionary these traditional readings have been restored to the Sunday liturgy. Strictly speaking, they belong to the first year of the three-year cycle, but for pastoral reasons may be used in the other years as well.

The gospel texts are of special importance. They are all from St John: *Jn 4:5-42* (The water of life); *Jn 9:1-41* (Baptism as enlightenment); *Jn 11:1-45* (Baptism as resurrection). They are instructive not only for the catechumens but for us, the baptised, as well. In a real sense we are all learners, mere apprentices in the Christian life. The Church makes use of the liturgy to teach us about the mysteries of our faith. Baptism, by which we are inserted into the body of Christ, is a sacrament which we may never take for granted.

Of particular interest on these Sundays of Lent is the unified theme presented by the liturgy. The Church has arranged that the readings and other texts proper to these Sundays all in some way converge on the message of the gospel. The theme may be announced in the entrance antiphon or opening prayer, fore-shadowed in the Old Testament reading, taken up again in the preface and echoed in the communion antiphon.

Let us now take a look at these Sunday readings with the intention of drawing from them all that they have to teach us about the sacrament of baptism and our life in Christ which follows from it.

The water of life. On this third Sunday of Lent the three readings of the Mass allude to water, the symbol of baptism. In the passage from Exodus *(17:3-7)* we recall how Moses struck the rock in the desert. He struck it with his staff and water flowed from it for all the people to drink.

In the second reading *(Rm 5:1-2, 5-8)* St Paul uses the analogy of water to describe the action of the Holy Spirit in our lives: "The love of God has been poured into our hearts by the Holy Spirit which has been given us."

The gospel *(Jn 4:5-42)* recounts our Lord's discourse with the Samaritan woman at the well of Sychar. He tells her about a mysterious gift of water which he has to offer: it is God's gift; whoever drinks it will never thirst again; it will become a spring inside one, welling up to eternal life.

The fathers of the Church have explained this gospel in the context of Christian baptism. It lends itself very well to a baptismal interpretation, and that is how the catechumens of old would have understood it. This we ourselves may legitimately do, without, however, interpreting it too narrowly in this sense. For the "gift of God" and the "living water" represent not just a sacrament but Christ himself. "Living water" in the Old Testament symbolises wisdom and truth, the riches contained in revelation. Here it refers to the life-giving teaching of Christ, who is incarnate wisdom. It is Christ's revelation of himself and must be assimilated. Here the action of the Holy Spirit comes into play: only then will it become a "spring inside him, welling up to eternal life".[5]

In this gospel Christ shows himself to be an excellent teacher.

He is patient with the woman whom he meets at the well. He begins by arousing her curiosity and then leads her step by step to the knowledge that he is the Christ. The request for a drink of water was but a pretext to disclose to her the gift of God. It was really the woman's faith that he sought, according to St Augustine, whose homily on this gospel we should read in the office of readings for this Sunday (*Divine Office*, II, pp. 146-48).

Notice how the preface echoes this thought of St Augustine and develops it:

> When he asked the woman of Samaria
> for water to drink,
> Christ had already prepared for her
> the gift of faith.
> In his thirst to receive her faith
> he awakened in her heart the fire of your love.

Faith and baptism are closely related. Baptism is a sacrament of faith. If we are already baptised let us give thanks for the gift of God and pray for an ever deepening faith.

Baptism as enlightenment. On the fourth Sunday of Lent the theme of light prevails. When one considers that one of the terms for baptism in the early Church was enlightenment *(photismos)*, it is clear that the readings, especially the gospel, have been very aptly chosen.

The ritual of baptism includes an anointing as well as a washing or immersion in water. This is reflected in the first reading from the first book of Samuel *(16:1, 6-7, 10-13)* which describes the anointing of David as king of Israel. This harmonises with the gospel text in which there is also an anointing: Jesus anoints the eyes of the blind man with clay and spittle and sends him to wash in the Pool of Siloam where his sight is restored.

Between these two readings we have a text from St Paul *(Eph 5:8-14)* in which light is not only a symbol of baptism but of the whole Christian life. At the end of this reading we have what appears to be a fragment of an early baptismal hymn: ''Wake up from your sleep, rise from the dead, and Christ will shine on you.'' But it is the gospel *(Jn 9:1-41)* which commands our attention. Here Jesus makes his great claim that he is ''the light of the world''.

The Church fathers saw in the pool of Siloam a symbol of the baptismal font in which men, blinded by ignorance and sin, have their sight restored and begin to know God as he really is. Here is how St Augustine comments on this text in one of his homilies:[6]

> The blind man represents the human race. This blindness was, in the first man, the result of original sin, and it has communicated to us all, not only the seed of death, but also that of iniquity. . . He (the blind man) washed in the pool which is interpreted ''sent''; he was baptised in Christ. . . Let them (the catechumens) then hasten unto this pool of salvation, if they seek the light.

Faith and baptism are so closely associated that the symbol of light relates to both. The convert is one who ''sees the light'', that is, he is drawn by the gift of faith to the knowledge of God. In the sacrament of baptism he is further ''enlightened'', receiving the light of grace. This light, which is given to us here below through faith and baptism, will be perfected in heaven in that vision of God which is called the ''light of glory''. St Augustine contemplates this aspect of the gospel in his homily given in the breviary for this Sunday *(Divine Office* II, pp. 173-74).

Baptism as resurrection. On the fifth Sunday of Lent the theme is resurrection and new life. In the first reading *(Ez 37:12-14)* the prophet Ezekiel foretells the return of his people from exile under the image of a resurrection. In the second reading *(Rm 8:8-11)* St Paul speaks explicitly of the resurrection of our bodies through ''the Spirit of him who raised Jesus from the dead''.

The gospel *(Jn 11:1-45)* recounts the miracle of the raising of Lazarus. It is a gospel we are very familiar with since it occurs so often at funeral Masses. On the occasion of a personal bereavement we draw comfort from those great words: ''I am the resurrection. If anyone believes in me, even though he dies he

21

will live, and whoever lives and believes in me will never die.''

In this gospel we see Jesus at his most human (weeping at the grave of Lazarus) and at his most divine (working his greatest miracle in raising Lazarus). This thought is also evoked in the preface:

> As a man like us, Jesus wept for Lazarus
>   his friend.
> As the eternal God, he raised Lazarus
>   from the dead.

The next line of the preface connects the gospel with the new life conferred through baptism:

> Christ gave us the sacraments to lift us up
>   to everlasting life.

We will now briefly explore this connection between the raising of Lazarus and the mystery of baptism.[7]

The raising of Lazarus is a *sign* of the resurrection of Jesus. It is a miracle which reveals his power over life and death; it authenticates his claim to be the resurrection and the life. It is also a sign of our own future resurrection through our union with Christ.

It is faith which establishes that union with Christ who is the source of our resurrection. Jesus leads Martha to an ever deeper faith in himself, and each question elicits from her a more explicit act of faith. That is the response required of all of us if we are to enter fully into the life which Christ brings.

Baptism puts the seal to our faith. Through faith and baptism we already share in the life of the risen Christ. This is the great mystery which we will celebrate at Easter, in the light of the Resurrection itself. That mystery is symbolised and fore-shadowed in the raising of Lazarus.

The sacrament of faith. When one compares the three readings from the gospel of St John which we have discussed above, a similar pattern emerges: an encounter, a discourse, a sign and a profession of faith.

22

Reminders of baptism. Certain devotional practices and familiar prayers have an association with baptism, and so may be employed as reminders of our baptism.

When we make the sign of the cross we recall the day of our baptism when we received this sign ''on our foreheads and in our hearts''. It is as though Christ took possession of us by this sign. In tracing it on the child's forehead, the priest says: ''In its name I claim you for Christ our Saviour by the sign of his cross.'' To make this sign slowly and reverently would be one good way of recalling our baptism during Lent.

The use of holy water is a very obvious reminder of baptism. To use it as a conscious reminder of this sacrament is an effective way of renewing the grace of our baptism. The Church has now introduced the blessing of holy water into the ritual of the Mass. It may replace the penitential rite. The water is blessed, the sacrament of baptism is recalled and the people are sprinkled. It would be very fitting if on the Sundays of Lent, especially the third, fourth and fifth when the Liturgy of the Word makes special reference to baptism, that this simple rite of blessing and sprinkling would be used as a collective recalling of baptism.

The Apostles' Creed and the ''Our Father'' are two important prayers closely associated with baptism. The former is a baptismal profession of faith. It expresses in summary form all the articles of Christian faith. It reminds us that we have received the sacrament of faith and that we are called upon to make our lives a living expression of that faith. The Lord's Prayer, or ''Our Father'', is the prayer *par excellence* of the baptised; it is the prayer of those who have received the ''spirit of adoption'' and may address God as Father. Christians of antiquity made a point of reciting it thrice daily. St Cyprian said this about it:

> What deep mysteries, my dearest brothers, are contained in the Lord's prayer! How many and great they are! They are expressed in a few words but they are rich in spiritual power so that nothing is left out; every petition and prayer we have to make is included. It is a compendium of heavenly doctrine *(Divine Office* III, p. 194; office of readings for Monday, week 11 of year).

23

In each incident Jesus makes a great claim. To the Samaritan woman he offers "living water" and declares that he is the Messiah; to the man healed of his blindness he reveals that he is "the light of the world". To Martha he makes the greatest claim of all: "I am the resurrection."

It is revealing to compare the different responses Jesus meets with. The Samaritan woman by her very questioning expresses the beginning of faith: "I wonder if he is the Christ." The man healed of blindness makes a silent profession of faith: he falls down and worships Christ. Martha goes even further in her response of faith: "Yes, Lord, I believe that you are the Christ, the Son of God, the one who was to come into the world."

Christ offers us light, truth and eternal life; he offers us a share in his own divine life. In return he looks for the response of faith. That response is all-important. It is especially important in those preparing for baptism, but Lent is a time for all of us to awaken and deepen our faith.

NOTES

1. J. Boutei, H. Bourgeois, "The Catechumenate in France Today" in *Becoming a Catholic Christian,* edited by W. Reedy (Sadlier, New York, 1979), pp. 10-21.
2. *Ordo Initiationis Christianae Adultorum.* An interim English translation of this Ordo has been made by ICEL. See commentary by A. Kavanagh, OSB, "The Norm of Baptism: The New Rite of Christian Initiation of Adults" in *Worship* 48, March 1974, pp. 143-52.
3. See A. Kavanagh, *The Shape of Baptism* (Pueblo, New York, 1978), p. 104.
4. See his article, "The Rite of Christian Initiation of Adults at Ten Years" in *Worship* 56 (July 1982), p. 311.
5. See commentary of I. de la Potterie, "Jésus et les Samiritains" in *Assemblées du Seigneur* 16, Editions du Cerf, Paris, 1969, pp. 34-49.
6. Homily 44 on the Gospel of St John.
7. See commentary of M. Morlet, "Le Dernier Signe de la Glorification de Jésus" in *Assemblées du Signeur* 18, pp. 11-25.

3

LENT AND PENANCE

Penance as conversion. The reception of ashes at the beginning of Lent recalls the time when public penitents wore sack-cloth and ashes as a sign of their repentance. Since about the tenth century it has been the custom for all the faithful to receive ashes on their foreheads on this first day of Lent. This ceremony manifests the Church's willingness to undergo penance. It is as though all of us, from the Pope down, were included among the ranks of the public penitents.

It is important that we have a clear idea of what penance means. Too easily we equate it with some of its external expressions, for example, fasting and abstinence. These are indeed manifestations of penance but they do not constitute the full reality. The Christian notion of penance goes much deeper than that. Let us try to understand it in the light of sacred scripture and the Church's teaching.

Penance is one of the constant themes of both Old and New Testaments. The Greek word for penance, *metanoia,* conveys the idea of conversion or change of heart. This implies that penance involves an inner change in man, a turning to God, a re-orientation of our lives towards God. It also implies a turning away from sin, a rejection of all that was evil in our lives. Penance affects us at the very roots of our being.

This change of heart or conversion presupposes a *call* from God. It is he who calls us and gives us the grace to respond. During the season of Lent the Church will often pray for the grace of conversion, as, for example, in this prayer for Monday of the first week:

Turn our hearts back to you, God our saviour;
form us by your heavenly teaching,
so that we may truly profit by our Lenten
   observance.

This conversion need not be sudden or dramatic, as it was with St Paul or St Augustine. It may be gradual and imperceptible, an ongoing activity in our lives. The call to conversion is always there and so our response must be continuous.

The presence of sin in our lives makes penance or conversion necessary at all times. If we feel that we have nothing whatever to reproach ourselves with, we should listen to the blunt words of St John:

If we say we have no sin in us, we are deceiving ourselves and refusing to admit the truth *(1 Jn 1:8).*

Penance, in the sense of conversion, is never optional. Even when we have long since resolved to give our lives for God, our conversion is never complete and total. There remain corners of our heart never fully converted to the Gospel, pockets of resistance to God's grace; we have always to contend with our limitations and failures. Only God can create a new heart within us. This is true even in the lives of very holy people. In his short study, *Spiritual Exodus,* Philip Boyce highlights three salient graces or conversions in the lives of John Henry Newman and St Thérèse of Lisieux.[1]

In the lives of those who have estranged themselves from God through grave sin, conversion is all the more urgent. When God in his mercy bestows on them the grace of conversion they must not delay in responding to his grace. Moral inertia and cowardice will suggest a thousand reasons for delay; one recalls the plea of the young Augustine: "Lord, grant me continence, *but not yet.*"

There are times when the voice of God calling us to repentance is more pressing and insistent than at others. The season of Lent is a time when the whole Church is called to penance and conversion. It is a God-given opportunity to undertake the conversion of our hearts. In the words of scripture, quoted in the liturgy of Ash Wednesday:

> At the favourable time, I have listened to you; on the day of salvation I came to your help. Well, now is the favourable time; this is the day of salvation (2 Cor 6:2).

And in the words of the psalmist which we hear at the beginning of the daily office: "O that today you would listen to his voice!"

The practice of penance. While the essence of penance consists in a sincere change of heart, it also requires visible expression in our life and conduct. This leads us to speak of the "observance of Lent" and the traditional penitential exercises which are associated with this season.

The practice of penance does not entail doing extraordinary things. Life has its own built-in penances, and normally the best way of exercising this virtue is to humbly and patiently accept what used to be called the "duties of our state in life". In the Introduction to the Rite of Penance (3 and 4), we are told that the Church must constantly pursue repentance and renewal; and this she accomplishes by sharing in the sufferings of Christ, enduring difficulties, carrying out works of mercy and charity, and adopting ever more fully the outlook of the Gospel.

We may sum up the whole Lenten observance in a single word, and this is the word "service": a more perfect service of God and of neighbour; service of God in prayer, worship, self-denial and a more active faith; service of our fellow human-beings in a greater readiness to respond to their needs.

To put it in another way, our Lenten observance consists in giving and forgiving. We must give not only external things such as money and possessions, but also such precious things as our time and sympathy, making ourselves available to other people even when that may cause us serious inconvenience.

We must also forgive. The practice of mutual pardon is all-important and we are reminded of it again and again in the liturgy. Two important gospel texts confront us with this message during the first week of Lent. The first, read on Tuesday, recounts our Lord's teaching of the "Our Father" to his disciples *(Mt 6:7-15)*. This passage contains not only the formula of the Lord's Prayer but also the very important addition on the necessity of mutual pardon:

> Yes, if you forgive others their failings, your heavenly Father will forgive you yours; but if you do not forgive others, your Father will not forgive your failings either.

Then on Friday of the first week the gospel *(Mt 5:20-26)* instructs us on the need to be reconciled with our offended brother before we bring our offering to the altar.

In one of his Lenten sermons Pope St Leo added his own reflections to this gospel message. Easter, he said, is the feast of divine pardon; it celebrates man's reconciliation with God through the sacrifice of Christ. It is appropriate that we prepare for it by pardoning one another and being reconciled with those estranged from us.[2]

In the liturgy of the Orthodox Church, the Sunday before Lent is known as the "Sunday of Forgiveness". It includes a special ceremony of mutual forgiveness at the end of Vespers on Sunday evening, thus showing that "there can be no true fast, no genuine repentance, no reconciliation with God, unless we are at the same time reconciled with one another".[3]

Fasting, almsgiving and prayer. Among the traditional works of penance, special importance has always been attached to fasting, almsgiving and prayer. Already in the Old Testament these practices were highly valued. They are so closely related as to form a kind of unity.

Fasting during Lent, however, has been greatly modified. We are now obliged to fast on two days only: Ash Wednesday and Good Friday.[4] We are encouraged to fast throughout the whole of Lent, but this is a counsel and not a commandment. For some this is a sign that the Church has abandoned penance and that practices such as fasting have been set aside.

The Church has not done so, but in mitigating the fast she is motivated by pastoral considerations. Not all are equal to the rigours of a prolonged fast. Health, age and the kind of work in which people are engaged have to be considered. The Church today therefore requires of all the faithful only a bare minimum of fasting.

But the example of Christ himself, the constant tradition of the Church and the abiding need for penance do not permit us simply to ignore fasting. It continues as an important element of Christian asceticism, an ideal not only to be valued but also realised to some degree by all of us.

Let us consider for a moment the purpose of the fast. It would be a mistake to consider it merely in a negative sense. It has been truly observed that ''our self-denial is the path that leads to our self-affirmation''.[5] The fast is not an end in itself. It is good to practise moderation and restraint, but these are not specifically Christian virtues. The fast must have a higher purpose: its ultimate object is not the subjugation of the body and its appetites but, rather, more perfect love of God and neighbour.

The prophets and Christ himself have warned against the dangers of mere formalism. Where love is absent no amount of fasting will please God. This is trenchantly expressed in the words of Isaiah, read at Mass on the Friday after Ash Wednesday:

> Is not this the sort of fast that pleases me — it is the Lord who speaks — to break unjust fetters and undo the thongs of the yoke, to let the oppressed go free, and break every yoke, to share your bread with the hungry and shelter the homeless poor *(Is 58:6-7)*.

Fasting, if it is to measure up to the ideal expressed in the prophets and the gospels, must be completed by generous acts of practical charity.

There is a close connection between fasting and almsgiving. This is an idea which has been rediscovered in recent years, and one which gives a whole new motivation to our fast. What is saved by restricting ourselves in food, luxuries, entertainment, etc., is given away as alms to the poor. This is known as ''the fast of sharing'', and is widely practised by families and religious communities today.

This idea was often expressed in the writings of the fathers, for example Pope St Leo and Pope St Gregory the Great. It is also witnessed to in the texts of the Lenten liturgy. Let us take a few examples. The office of readings during Lent has two fine sermons relating fasting with almsgiving. The first, read on Monday of the first week, is by St Gregory Nazianzen. In it he exhorts us, as good stewards of God's gifts, to show kindness and love to all people, but especially to the poor. Then on Tuesday of the third week we have that beautiful sermon of St Peter Chrysologus, which begins:

> There are three things, brethren, three, through which faith stands firm, devotion abides, and virtue endures; prayer, fasting and mercy. What prayer knocks for upon a door, fasting successfully begs and mercy receives. Prayer, fasting and mercy: these three are a unit. They give life to one another. For fasting is the soul of prayer; and mercy is the life of fasting.

There are so many worthy causes to which we can contribute: the St Vincent de Paul Society, for example, and organisations for assistance to under-developed nations and for the relief of famine, such as Trócaire. What we save from our self-imposed fasts, from our restrictions in such things as alcohol, tobacco, entertainment, etc., we should put to generous use. This requires a very real spirit of sacrifice.

St Raymund of Penafort had a great love for the poor. He liked to call them his creditors. It is in this spirit that we should assist the poor. Our Lenten fast should not be merely an exercise in thrift. Like St Raymund, we should regard the money we have saved as belonging by right to the poor. We are their debtors.

Lent has also been likened to a retreat or mission; not just a parish or community retreat, but a retreat for the whole Church. In a retreat we set aside as much time as possible for prayer. Likewise, in this Lenten retreat the Church's prayer is more intense and continuous.

There is a close kinship between prayer and fasting. In the gospel for the first Sunday of Lent *(Mt 4:1-11)*, which describes the temptation of Jesus, our Lord rebukes Satan who challenged him to change the stones into loaves of bread: "Man does not live on bread alone but on every word that comes from the mouth of God." The word of God is also food, it is the bread of life. It is *cibus cibo melior,* food more substantial than food itself, to quote an inscription found on a monastic lectern. To the extent that we abstain from material food, our souls should hunger more and more for this spiritual food.

In the celebration of Mass, the faithful are nourished both at the table of God's word and at the table of his sacrament; word and Eucharist are complementary forms of sustenance. The Mass is our sacrifice, our nourishment and our greatest prayer. And so among the traditional practices of Lent, that of daily attendance at Mass and communion deserves the highest recommendation.[6]

Listening to the word of God is an essential part of prayer. It is very important to be open and receptive to the word of God. It is a word which is alive and efficacious. How well this is expressed in the text from Isaiah which is read at Mass on Tuesday of the first week:

> Yes, as the rain and the snow come down from the heavens and do not return without watering the earth, making it yield and giving growth to provide seed for the sower and bread for the eating, so the word that goes from my mouth does not return to me empty, without carrying out my will and succeeding in what it was sent to do *(Is 55:10-11).*

During the six weeks of Lent the Liturgy of the Word, both in the Eucharist and the prayer of the hours, is especially abundant and varied. We have but to listen to it, reflect on it in our hearts and allow it to act upon us.

Prayer is a dialogue in which listening is as important as speaking. As partners in the dialogue, we must be sensitive and receptive to the voice of God. This has been described as the "art of conversing with Jesus" *(The Imitation of Christ),* and there is a prayer in the new Roman missal which expresses this concisely and with feeling. It is from the second Sunday of Lent and is obviously inspired by the gospel of the day which tells of the transfiguration of Christ:

> God our Father
> you bid us listen to your Son, the well-beloved.
> Nourish our hearts on your word,
> purify the eyes of our mind (*Breviary* version).

What Christ asks of us in prayer may be difficult: we may be required to renounce this or to undertake that. The word of God is indeed a "two-edged sword"; that is why we may be rather afraid of prayer. The fact that it is demanding makes it an effective part of our penance. True conversion of heart presupposes a willingness on our part to hear and to heed what God asks of us. Our attitude should be: "Speak, Lord, for your servant is listening."

In the dialogue which is prayer, we can also address the Father through and in his Son or speak directly to Christ. Prayer, founded on faith in Christ, is always efficacious. Tertullian expresses this belief in a bold phrase found in the office of readings for Thursday of the third week of Lent: "Prayer alone it is that conquers God." In the gospel for Thursday of the first week, we have Christ's own promise: "Ask, and it will be given to you; search, and you will find; knock, and the door will be opened to you" *(Mt 7:7).*

In a season of penance it is natural that we should pray for pardon, pardon for our own sins and for those of others. We make our own the humble admission of guilt which Daniel uttered on behalf of his people: "We have sinned, we have done wrong, we have acted wickedly, we have betrayed your commandments and your ordinances" *(Dn 9:4-10*, read at Mass on Monday of the second week). The great prayer of Moses pleading for his rebellious people is also a fitting expression of the Church's prayer: "Lord, why should your wrath blaze against this people of yours whom you brought out of the land of Egypt? . . . Leave your burning wrath; relent and do not bring this disaster on your people" (*Ex 32:7-14*, read at Mass on Thursday of fourth week). There are other beautiful Old Testament prayers in the readings for Lent, for example, the humble prayer of repentance on Tuesday of the third week (*Dn 3: 35. 34-43)*, containing the well-known line: "May the contrite soul, the humbled spirit be acceptable to you . . .".

A Lenten triad:

> Prayer, which is joined to fasting and almsgiving is good, for almsgiving will purge away every sin. . . (*Tob 12:8-9,* the responsory for Wednesday of the third week).

Fasting supplies us with the means to practise almsgiving. It is also conducive to prayer. It increases our hunger for God's word and sacrament, and for God himself. Note how the prayers of the Mass express this thought: "Through the discipline of Lent help us to grow in our desire for you" (Opening prayer, Tuesday of first week); "May we who receive this sacrament restrain our earthly desires and grow in love for the things of heaven" (Prayer after communion, same day).

On the third Sunday of Lent we have the following short prayer which sums up all that we have been saying on the subject of fasting, almsgiving and prayer:

> Father, you have taught us to overcome our sins by prayer, fasting and works of mercy. When we are discouraged by our weakness, give us confidence in your love.

The sacrament of reconciliation. The 1973 Order of Penance strongly recommends the practice of sacramental confession at this season. In article 13 it states:

> The season of Lent is most appropriate for celebrating the sacrament of penance. Already on Ash Wednesday the people of God hear the solemn invitation, "Turn away from sin and believe the good news". It is therefore fitting to have several celebrations during Lent, so that all the

faithful may have an opportunity to be reconciled with God and their neighbour and so to be able to celebrate the paschal mystery in the Easter triduum with renewed hearts.

The sacrament of penance, or reconciliation, has been instituted expressly for the forgiveness of sins. Through the ministry of the priest, who acts in the name of Christ and through his power, God's pardon is bestowed on the penitent who confesses his sins and is rightly disposed.

Among the works of penance carried out during Lent, this sacrament holds a unique place. Just as the Eucharist is the "centre and summit" of all the Church's liturgical actions, the sacrament of reconciliation is the crowning of all our penitential acts. It consecrates all our efforts to turn from sin and be reconciled with our neighbour and with God. It must not be thought of as just one extra good work added to our prayer, fasting and acts of charity, but as a privileged and grace-filled moment, a high-point in our ascent to God.

During Lent, Christ, through the Holy Spirit, is at work in the hearts of men and women, leading them to conversion of heart and renewal of their lives. The experience of God's merciful love moves the penitent to hate sin and to want to return love for love. A gradual transformation takes place in the soul which, if authentic, will seek to express itself exteriorly in the various forms we have described. It is here that the sacrament of reconciliation enters in and plays its providential role. In the words of the 1976 Canadian Bishops' pastoral, "The sacramental celebration seals and blesses the love which is there already, and raises it to be a public sign of Christ's love and forgiveness."[7]

Forms of celebration: individual and communal. Elsewhere I have written: "I believe that the two forms of penance, individual and communal, will exist side by side. They will even help one another because in our prayer and sacramental life we need the personal element and we need the community or social element.

34

God calls each one of us by name but he calls us along with our brothers and sisters.''[8]

Let us now briefly consider the rites for the celebration of the sacrament as proposed in the revised Order of Penance. These are: 1) reconciliation of individual penitents; 2) reconciliation of several penitents with individual confession and absolution; 3) reconciliation of several penitents with general confession and absolution.

Reconciliation of individual penitents. It is well known that Pope John Paul II is very committed to upholding this traditional form of penance. We are now familiar with the almost prophetic gesture whereby, on occasion, he will enter the confessional in St Peter's and hear confessions like any other pastoral priest. This strongly reinforces his verbal exhortations. In the words that follow we see the importance he attaches to the personal element in the sacraments, particularly in this one: "In this sacrament of penance we are invited to meet Christ personally and to do so frequently." And then, recalling what he said in his first encyclical, he adds: "In faithfully observing the centuries old practice of individual confession with a personal act of sorrow and the intention to amend and make satisfaction, the Church is thereby defending the human soul's individual right — man's right — to a more personal encounter with the crucified and forgiving Christ, with Christ saying through the minister of the sacrament, 'Your sins are forgiven'.''[9]

People should be encouraged at least once during Lent to avail of this form of sacramental penance. It should not be left to the last moment of the last hurried days of Holy Week. It should be carefully prepared with the seriousness which is proper to a sacrament. After all, this is a special occasion, not just a routine performance of piety. It should be calm, unhurried and prayerful, a true dialogue with the priest who represents Christ as judge, healer and counsellor.

Reconciliation of several penitents with individual confession. Penance is the way back to God, and along that route there are other fellow travellers to keep us company. In a community

35

celebration we help one another by listening to the word of God together, by examining our consciences together, by praying together. In the words of the introduction to the Rite of Penance: "A community celebration brings out the ecclesial nature of penance. All the faithful hear the word of God together, and they are all invited to change their lives by God's mercy" (no. 22).

Such celebrations remind us that our sins are not only an offence against God but also against his Church, and since the Church is the body of Christ, it follows that the lives of its members interact. No man is an island! The good we do rebounds to the benefit of the whole Church-organism, the sins we commit impair and diminish its life.

Again, such celebrations turn the spotlight on social evils for which we all, to some extent, share responsibility. This corporate dimension of sin is a perfectly biblical concept and we meet it in a number of the readings during Lent.[10] It is good for us to be reminded that we are accountable not only for our own personal sins, but also as a people, as a Church, for much that is wrong in the society in which we live. We tend to ignore, or to blame others (the government) for injustices such as discrimination against minority groups, gross neglect of weaker members of the community — the poor, old age pensioners etc. The Christian attitude is to look into our own hearts and not to shirk responsibility.

A practical difficulty in organising a communal celebration of penance is the need to have a number of priests at hand to hear the individual confessions. It is estimated that one priest to ten penitents is the optimum ratio. Such availability of clergy may appear utopian. On the other hand, with good co-operation and a sharing of manpower among the neighbouring parishes, the obstacles are not insurmountable. The services can be held in the different churches on a rota basis.

We should not overlook the possibility of holding non-sacramental communal "Penitential Services". These are provided for in the appendix to the Rite of Penance. These can be organised with little difficulty, even in the absence of a priest, in a parish or religious community. They are by no means to be under-valued. For one thing, they help to maintain and foster

36

the spirit of penance and conversion which should be the permanent attitude of a Christian. Moreover, as Fr Donal Murray points out in his book *The Inner Truth,* such services are not entirely non-sacramental. The whole of life is sacramental because the sacraments express the deepest truth about that life. And so "if we diminish the variety and richness of popular devotions and para-liturgical acts, as we have perhaps tended to do in recent years, we impoverish the sacramental celebrations too because we have less to bring to the sacraments".[11]

Two penitential services for the season of Lent are given as samples. If the sacrament is to be conferred in the course of the celebration, then the individual confessions followed by individual absolutions take place after the readings and homily. For a further sample of a penitential service readers may wish to consult the review *Scripture in Church,* no. 45 (1982): "A Communal Celebration of the Sacrament of Reconciliation during Lent" by Conor O'Riordan, OP.

Reconciliation of several penitents with general absolution. This is the controversial Rite Three of the Order of Penance. Its use is restricted by the conditions laid down in articles 31 to 34 of the Introduction. Authorisation for its use depends on the bishop of the diocese in consultation with his fellow-bishops. As a condition for its employment there must be a serious pastoral necessity, such as would arise when and where there was a lack of priests to hear confessions properly within a suitable period of time, thus depriving penitents of sacramental grace and perhaps of holy communion for a long time.

NOTES

1. Vol. 6 of *Living Flame Series,* Carmelite Centre of Spirituality, Dublin, 1979.
2. Sermon 50, quoted by G. Hudon in *La Perfection Chrétienne d'après les Sermons de Saint Léon,* Editions du Cerf, Paris, 1959, p. 215.
3. *The Lenten Triodion,* translated by Mother Mary and Kallistos Ware; Faber & Faber, London, 1978, p. 47.
4. In the early Church, before the institution of Lent, a rigorous fast was observed only on the two days before Easter. This was the paschal fast, an

integral part of the Easter celebration. In the Liturgy Constitution of Vatican II, art. 110, an attempt was made to return to this ancient observance: ''But the paschal fast must be kept sacred. Let it be celebrated everywhere on Good Friday, and where possible be *prolonged throughout Holy Saturday* so that the joys of the Sunday may be attained with uplifted and clear mind.''

5.   *The Lenten Triodion,* already cited, pp. 27-28.

6.   In the early centuries public celebration of Mass was normally reserved to Sundays and greater feasts. This tradition was maintained in Rome for a long time. An exception was made, however, for the season of Lent. Between the sixth and eighth centuries in Rome the practice of daily Mass celebrated by the pope or his delegate became established. This included a solemn procession and full participation by the people. The Roman Missal, now in use, encourages bishops to celebrate Mass in different churches of their dioceses during Lent; an idea inspired by the Roman ''stational'' liturgy.

7.   Published in *National Bulletin on Liturgy,* vol. 9, no. 52 (1976), and in *Notitiae* 121-22 (1976), pp. 334-354. This citation, p. 344.

8.   ''The New Rites of Penance'' in *Supplement to Doctrine and Life,* No. 67 (1977), p. 8.

9.   Quoted by J. Adamson, OSB in *Faith* (Nov.-Dec. 1981), pp. 24-25.

10.   See M. Maher, MSC, ''The Lenten Lectionary'' in *Scripture in Church,* No. 38, pp. 371-380, especially p. 378.

11.   This book is published by Veritas, Dublin, 1980. The citation is from p. 7. The first three chapters of this book will be found relevant for our theme.

12.   See Eoin de Bhaldraithe, OCSO, ''Communal Absolution'' in *The Furrow* (November 1976), pp. 626-27.

13.   See reply of Sacred Congregation for the doctrine of the Faith of 20 January 1978. Text in *Notitiae* 138 (1978), pp. 6-7; also cited with brief commentary by A. Flannery, OP in *Doctrine and Life* (April 1978), pp. 241-42.

4

SUNDAY PREACHING DURING LENT

The lectionary, with its three-year cycle of readings for Sundays, enables the preacher to vary his approach from year to year. Not that the programme of readings is substantially different in years A, B and C for the Lenten cycle; but each of these has characteristic features, suggests specific themes and so provides a particular approach through Lent to Easter.

There is a common framework for the three years of the cycle. The first Sunday of Lent has the gospel account of the Temptation of Jesus, according to Matthew, Mark and Luke respectively. The other readings are variable. On the second Sunday the scene is Mount Thabor and we consider the mystery of the Transfiguration. With these two great gospel narratives the Lenten season has been inaugurated and set in progress.

It is within the middle portion of Lent that the differences occur. For the third, fourth and fifth Sundays, the scripture readings, including the gospels, constitute distinctive units of their own. Thus in year A, as we have already observed in chapter two, it is the baptismal motif which is prominent: all three readings for each of these Sundays relate in one way or other to the sacrament of baptism. In year B of the cycle, no clear-cut theme is discernible, but, as we shall see, the theme of God's *covenant* runs through the Old Testament readings for this particular year of Lent. And finally year C: here Sundays three to five provide readings which have clearly been chosen in relation to *penance* and *reconciliation* in the Christian life. And so we can sum up in the following simple plan:

> Year A: Baptism
> Year B.   The Covenant
> Year C: Penance and Reconciliation.

These will be treated of in turn. It should be said at the outset that these proposed headings are merely suggestive. The homilist is quite free to work out his own catechetical plan, based of course on the content of the lectionary.

It should also be noted that with the sixth Sunday (Palm Sunday) we have entered Holy Week, when the liturgy becomes again invariable, and all attention is focused on the final act in the mystery of redemption.

Having suggested themes for the Lenten cycle, let us now consider how we might develop these in a course of homilies.

Year A: Baptism. In the introductory chapter we described Lent as a journey in faith and conversion. In chapter two we sought to bring to light the baptismal elements in Lent, paying particular attention to the great "baptismal" gospels of Sundays three to five in year A. It is not necessary to recall what was said in those chapters. Here we avail of the faith-journey image to deepen our understanding of what becoming a Christian means.

The gospel of the first Sunday *(Mt 4:1-11),* recounting the temptation of Jesus after his forty days of fasting in the desert, recalls the forty years the Chosen People spent en route to the Promised Land. And the prayer of that Sunday is that we too may be led along the path of faith and understanding: "through our annual Lenten observance, Lord, deepen our understanding of the mystery of Christ." Lent is a pilgrimage of faith, a voyage of discovery in our understanding of who Christ is.

On this first Sunday we learn who Jesus really is: the true Son of God, who proves his sonship by his perfect fidelity, obedience, and by the exclusive worship he renders the Father. We, catechumens and baptised, also learn something about ourselves: that our faith will be put to the test, that we will be prey to doubt and discouragement, and possibly tempted to give up; but we are also assured of the divine protection, since Christ's victory is also ours.

On the following Sunday, in the gospel of the Transfiguration, we have a further revelation of Jesus as the Beloved Son. This experience of the majesty of God shining

40

through the humanity of Christ was intended to strengthen the faith of the apostles and to brace them for the coming crisis. This is an occasion for the homilist to show that the Christian experience is not all darkness: that God, in his consideration for our weakness, grants us glimpses of the invisible reality. If we are patient and persevere in prayer, we too will be granted from time to time a Thabor experience, intuitions of the glory that is in Christ, moments of ''unexpected re-assurance''.

The journey of faith continues. In the gospel for the third Sunday, Jesus reveals himself to the Samaritan woman as the ''living water'' and the ''saviour of the world''. On the fourth Sunday, again in a baptismal context, he is manifested as ''the light of the world'' *(Jn 9:1-41)*. And, finally, on the fifth Sunday, in the account of the raising of Lazarus *(Jn 11:1-45)*, Jesus declares: ''I am the resurrection. If anyone believes in me, even though he dies he will. . .''

We must help our people to advance along the path of faith, help them to re-discover their baptism and to renew their baptismal dedication to Christ. As Anne Field observes in her book, *New Life:* ''Today of course we do not have hundreds of converts from paganism to prepare for baptism each year. There are, however, many Christians to whom baptism meant very little until the Holy Spirit touched their lives, so that their first real commitment to following Christ was made only after many years of belonging to a Christian Church. This commitment has led to such a change in their lives that many of them consider themselves 'new' Christians.''

We would be wrong of course to underestimate the faith of ordinary Christians. Nor should we presume too much just because they were baptised and are practising. Rather we should take people as they are and try to help them progress towards a more mature and enlightened faith. That was Christ's way with people. Remember, the apostles themselves were slow learners; it was not till after the Resurrection, not fully until the day of Pentecost, that they finally saw the light. Is it any wonder then that our own progress in the faith is gradual and that difficulties are to be encountered on the way? This realisation should make us patient with ourselves and with others. It should help us to

41

understand better the problems of the young. Their questioning of religion need not be just negative; positively it may be the beginning of a *quest* which will lead ultimately to the truth. Young people must be helped to discover for themselves who Christ is, who God is. The season of Lent, leading up to the great profession of faith on Easter night, is a most opportune time to awaken and stimulate a faith that is dormant or none-too-strong.

Year B: The covenant theme. Baptism is not only a sacrament of faith, but also one of commitment. It is entry to a new way of life. This introduces us to the theme of the covenant which we could develop during these weeks of Lent.

It is through baptism that we enter, and are made sharers in, the New Covenant. Throughout Lent, by prayer and penance and listening to the word of God, we prepare ourselves for the renewal of that covenant in the course of the Easter celebrations. The renewal of baptismal promises could be seen as the *ceremony of covenant renewal.*

Admittedly, this idea of covenant, so fundamental in the Old Testament, is not an easy one to get across to people who have little acquaintance with scripture (and that includes many of our people). We can speak of it as an *agreement,* an agreement we enter into with God through Christ his Son. It is bi-lateral: on the one hand God offers us his love and protection, and, on the other, we offer him our faith, obedience and loyalty. A close relationship is established, expressed in the recurring promise: "You shall be my people, and I shall be your God."

Lent is a time for fostering this inter-personal relationship between God and ourselves. Not only must faith grow, but also our commitment to the things of faith. There must be a readier response to the Gospel and a more earnest following of Christ.

The priest, in his homilies, must encourage this response and foster this willingness to follow in the footsteps of the Master. Let him insist on the importance of prayer as a most effective means of building up a strong and permanent relationship with God. Without it, man remains estranged from his Creator and Father. As a result, the divine and human partners in the covenant become distanced from each other: a situation arises similar to that which sometimes arises in married life when the two partners, while living together, no longer relate to each other; a wall of silence has come between them.

Prayer, nourished by attentive listening to the word of God, this is what makes the covenant a reality in our lives. To foster this, we priests must make the most of the Lenten readings. A daily homily is recommended, whereby we break the bread of the word for our people just as we break for them the eucharistic bread, and as our Lord broke bread with the two travellers at Emmaus and opened for them the meaning of the scriptures.[2]

The covenant theme in the readings. In what follows I acknowledge my indebtedness to two Irish priests, Fr James Carroll and Fr Jack Murtagh (+ 1980), who suggested this approach to year B of Lent and explained it in the American review, *The Bible Today.*[3]

It is interesting to note that the Old Testament reading for each of the five Sundays leading up to Holy Week is connected with the covenant. What is more, there is a correspondence between these readings and those of the Easter Vigil where the covenant theme is again very prominent (these will be treated of in our commentary on the Vigil). Let us verify this:

First Sunday: God's covenant with Noah *(Gen 9:8-15)*. The first of the covenants with the promise that the earth would never be destroyed again by water. The sign of this promise is the rainbow.

Second Sunday: God's covenant with Abraham *(Gen 22:1-18)*. In reward for his faith and obedience, the patriarch receives the promise that his descendants will be as numerous as the stars of heaven, and that the nations will be blessed in him.

Third Sunday: The giving of the Law to Moses *(Gen 20:1-17)*. The commandments constitute the heart of the covenant. We must live by them if we truly wish to foster our relationship with God. They are the terms of the covenant to which we must constantly refer.

43

Fourth Sunday: The breaking of the covenant *(Chron 36:14-23).* In punishment for their sins the people are sent into exile. Sin ruptures the covenant. But even at this moment of disaster there is a promise of future restoration. God will remember his covenant.

Fifth Sunday: The promise of a *new covenant (Jer 31:31-34).* No longer a covenant set down on tablets of stone, but written in human hearts: "Deep within them I will plant my Law, writing it in their hearts. Then I will be their God and they shall be my people."

And so the convenant theme provides a pathway through Lent. It is worth noting that there is a progression in the sequence of readings leading from Noah and Abraham to the promise of a new and eternal covenant. This will be brought about by the sacrifice of Christ. He is the Mediator of the New Covenant who has become for all who obey him the "source of eternal salvation".

We can remind our congregations that it is through baptism that we, both as people of God and individually, enter into this covenant-agreement with the Father in Christ. The celebration of the Eucharist enables us to ratify and renew that covenant, as well as to receive its blessings. As Fr E.J. Breen remarks: "The Eucharist is the living celebration of salvation. It brings into our lives the same new covenant act of Jesus as the Last Supper."[4]

This approach would certainly be unusual, but has much in its favour. One of the principal aims of Lent is to prepare us for the celebration of the paschal mystery at Easter. Now the paschal Vigil constitutes the heart of the celebration. If, by concentrating on the Old Testament readings during Lent, we make the covenant something very real and relevant for our people, then we are initiating them into the great Good News of Easter night. The Liturgy of the Word and the renewal of baptismal promises, followed by Mass and communion, will all form part of a great ceremony of covenant renewal.

Year C: Penance and Reconciliation. The readings for Sundays three to five clearly suggest the theme of penance and reconciliation.

This of course is one of the major themes in Lent and has been treated of in the preceding chapter. It runs through all the week-day readings. But here in the heart of Lent, in the Sunday liturgy, the homilist has an opportunity to explore this subject in depth with his people, and to highlight particular aspects of it.[5] Let us first check the gospel passages:

3rd Sunday: Luke 13:1-9 (call to repentance, God's patience)

4th Sunday: Luke 15:1-3. 11-31 (parable of the "prodigal son")

5th Sunday: John 8:1-11 (Jesus pardons the adulteress).

It is surely not by accident that the selection from St Paul's writings admirably complements the gospel-text and provides an ideal commentary on it. The gospels proclaim God's patience, generosity, readiness to forgive, his initiative in restoring a friendship which had been lost. St Paul, addressing the Corinthians and Philippians, assures them that God's offer of pardon and reconciliation is a free gift to all sinners who turn in faith to Jesus Christ and are open to receive it.

The emphasis is on the divine initiative in the whole process of reconciliation. God's liberality, the extent to which he is prepared to go to restore the sinner to himself, defies all human comparison. While always respecting human freedom, it is he who sets in motion, even in the most wayward of his children, the process which leads from repentance to reconciliation. He is tender-hearted to the point of folly, but this is the "foolishness" of God which is so much wiser than human wisdom. And in the attitude of Jesus to sinners, the healing and restoring love of the Father is fully revealed.

It is also clear that human effort, always under the influence of grace, is required. As St Augustine somewhere says: "Man was redeemed without his co-operation, but he will not be saved without his co-operation." It is not enough for the prodigal son to indulge in vain regrets, he must decide to get up and leave this place and return to his father's house. It is not enough for us just to feel sorry for our sins, we must be willing to do penance and make our peace with God.

There can be no pact with sin, no peaceful co-existence with it. Jesus never condones it even when he is so full of mercy. He neither condones nor condemns. He hates sin but loves the sinner. What delicacy and tact he shows towards the woman accused of adultery: no accusation, no word of reproach, simply an invitation to her to begin her life anew, to face the future with newly-found hope.

If there is a note of warning and reproach in these readings, it is chiefly against human pride and complacency. In the Liturgy of the Word for the third Sunday, St Paul admonishes all of us when he says: "The man who thinks he is safe must be careful that he does not fall." Pride comes before a fall! Christ also, in the gospel of the day, strikes at our complacency and self-righteousness: "unless you repent you will all perish as they did".

Our preaching at this time could take the form of a collective examination of conscience. Certainly these readings amount to a critique of accepted attitudes to our erring brothers and sisters. What a contrast between the divine and the human attitude to the sinner and outcast, between the Christ-like and the pharisaical approach! Public opinion can be a cruel judge, and it is with dread that people ask themselves "what will the neighbours say?". A little more understanding and charity – for example to the unmarried mother – would spare a great deal of suffering. In a Christian society no-one should be socially ostracised.

In our examination of conscience we should ask ourselves: with which of the characters in these gospels do we identify? With the elder brother who begrudges the welcome accorded the young prodigal? With the pharisee only too ready to cast a stone? Is not that, to some extent, the attitude of all of us – too ready to disapprove and condemn? May we not also recognise ourselves in the prodigal son, for which of us has not squandered his inheritance, his endowments, his time, his talents, his opportunities for doing good? With him and with the repentant woman we should implore God's mercy.

46

We must begin to identify with the father in the parable, patient, persevering in hope, always on the look-out for the return of his son. We must imitate Christ who pardoned sinners and who on the cross cried out "Father, forgive them". This applies both to the individual members of the Church and to the community. The Church at every level should be a healing and a reconciling community. This is a responsibility of which people are to a great extent unaware; and yet it is clearly stated in the Order of Penance (no. 8) that "the whole Church, as a priestly people, has its part to play in the work of reconciliation entrusted to it". Lent is a favourable time when by prayer, good example and encouragement, we may help the fallen and the strays to make their peace with God and be restored to his friendship.

Let us remember that God has a heart larger and tenderer than man's heart, and that the Church, in the words of Archbishop Francois Marty of Paris, "is the reflection in this world of God's tenderness".

In conclusion, then, we may suggest the following themes for preaching:

1) God's patience inviting us to repentance.
2) Divine initiative. God's love preceded human effort.
3) Christ the revelation of the Father's redeeming love.
4) The ministry of reconciliation entrusted to the Church.
5) The Christian community as a healing, reconciling and welcoming body.

NOTES

1. *New Life* — what it meant to become a Christian in the early Church, Mowbray, London, 1978, p. 9.
2. References to the covenant theme are found in the Lenten readings, both scriptural and patristic; see first reading *(Genesis 17:3-9)* and psalm for Thursday of 5th week, and first reading for Saturday of same week *(Ezekiel 37:21-28)*. *Divine Office* II, Wednesday of first week, p. 105, and Friday of second week, p. 139 (Irenaeus on the Covenant of the Lord).
3. Title of articles, "Announcing the New Covenant" and "Preparing for Covenant Renewal" in *The Bible Today* (Feb. 1976), pp. 634-49.

5

LENT AND THE PASSION OF CHRIST

The theme of Christ's passion is never absent from the Lenten liturgy; it is there from the beginning, but gathers momentum as the weeks progress. We meet it in a hidden manner in the gospel of the first Sunday *(Mt 4: 1-11)* which describes the temptation of Jesus. There we see the Lord in his first open confrontation with Satan. The scene is set for the final struggle from which Christ will emerge victorious. He rejects all the allurements of the Prince of Darkness and chooses the way of obedience which will lead him to his passion and cross.

We meet the passion of Christ in an unexpected manner in the scene of the transfiguration, which provides the gospel reading for the second Sunday of Lent *(Mt 17: 1-9; Mk 9: 2-10; Lk 9: 28-36)*. The mystery of Christ's transfiguration was intended to strengthen the faith of the three chosen apostles, Peter, John and James; it was to prepare them for the passion and the "scandal of the cross". It is Luke who tells us that Moses and Elijah spoke to Christ "of his passing which he was to accomplish in Jerusalem". The preface of the second Sunday expands on this particular thought:

> On your holy mountain he revealed himself in glory in the presence of his disciples. He had already prepared them for his approaching death. He wanted to teach them through the Law and the Prophets that the promised Christ had first to suffer and so come to the glory of his resurrection.

In the readings for Friday of the second week we find a mysterious but express allusion to the death of Christ. In the Old Testament reading *(Gen 37:3-4, 12-13, 17-28)* it is foreshadow-

49

ed in the plot to kill Joseph. In the gospel *(Mt 21:33-43, 45-46)* Jesus foretells his own violent death in the parable of the vineyard and the wicked tenants who killed the son of the landowner.

Ascent to the cross. Jesus freely advances towards his sacrifice. Each evangelist underlines the voluntary character of his sufferings and sacrificial death. The idea of an ascent to the cross is suggested by St Matthew in his gospel read on Wednesday of the second week:

> Now we are going up to Jerusalem, and the Son of Man is about to be handed over to the chief priests and scribes. They will condemn him to death and will hand him over to the pagans to be mocked and scourged and crucified; and on the third day he will rise again *(Mt 20: 17-28).*

The final journey is an ascent to Jerusalem, to Calvary and, beyond the cross, to glory. It is an ascent and an ascension. St Luke expresses this with special clarity in his gospel *(Lk 9: 51):* "Now as the time drew near for him to be taken up to heaven, he resolutely took the road for Jerusalem and sent messengers ahead of him."

There is a great finality about that decision. Christ makes it in the clear foreknowledge of what lies ahead for him. The disciples are filled with forebodings, but for their master there can be no turning back: for this he came into the world.

Mounting opposition. During the fourth and fifth weeks of Lent the Church sets before us each day the gospel of St John. In the selected passages from chapters five to twelve we follow Christ, stage by stage, through the events leading up to his arrest and condemnation. St John conveys extremely well the atmosphere of tension and conflict. Christ is presented to us in daily confrontation with the Pharisees.

There is no dissimulation on Christ's part; he reveals who he is. He makes the great claim that he is one with the Father, that he is the Son of God. And it is this unequivocal assertion which arouses the fury of his accusers: "But that only made the Jews even more intent on killing him, because not content with breaking the sabbath, he spoke of God as his own Father, and so made himself God's equal" *(Jn 5:18; see also the gospel for Wednesday of fourth week)*.

The words of Christ evoke a response: fury on the part of his enemies, faith on the part of those who are prepared to listen and to take his words to heart. They are a challenge to us too. Christ addresses us in the gospels, eliciting from us the response of faith. The gospels are not a record of the past, but a living message to us men and women of today.

On Friday of the fourth week, the plot to kill Jesus is foretold in the first reading *(Wis 2:1, 12-22)*: "Let us condemn him to a shameful death." In the gospel *(Jn 7:1-2, 10, 25-30)*, Jesus again makes his great claim, and we are told that "they would have arrested him, but because his time had not yet come no one laid a hand upon him". His time had not yet come but was now imminent.

While the gospels describe the outward scene, other readings give us insights into what took place within the mind and heart of Christ. Here the Church makes use of Old Testament prophecies and the psalms and does so to great effect. For example, on Saturday of the fourth week Christ's attitude of total trust in the Father is admirably expressed in the words of Jeremiah *(11:18-20)*: "I for my part was like a trustful lamb being led to the slaughter-house, not knowing the schemes they were plotting against me."

The word "trustful" is the key to his feelings. He accepts his Father's will unconditionally and with total trust. The psalms, with their constant note of trust in all human circumstances, are suitable for expressing the feelings of Christ on the eve of his passion. Take, for example, Psalm 7 which is used as a responsorial psalm during this time: "Lord, God, I take refuge in you. From my pursuer save me and rescue me", and then the note of confidence: "God is the shield that protects me, who saves the upright of heart."

The imitation of Christ. The passion of Christ is not just an object of contemplation, but also a programme of Christian living. It is

51

summed up in those words of the Lord: "If anyone wants to be a follower of mine, let him renounce himself and take up his cross and follow me" *(Mt 12:24)*. This call to renunciation is repeated again and again in the New Testament writings, as for example in the first letter of Peter (*2:21*, RSV version): "For to this you have been called, because Christ also suffered for you, leaving for you an example, that you should follow in his steps."

The office of readings is especially rich in this regard. The patristic readings show us how the great fathers of the Church have understood and expanded upon this idea of the *imitatio Christi*. The first father I would cite is St Augustine in his commentary on Psalm 140, read on Tuesday of the second week (*Divine Office* II, pp. 128-29). He shows how Christ must continue to suffer in his Church until the end of time. St Paul was of course very conscious of the Church's participation in the sufferings of Christ, especially in his own life. It is a very basic message of Christian morality.

St Gregory the Great, in his commentary on the book of Job, read on Friday of the third week (*Divine Office* II, p. 167) has this to say: "If the mystery of the Lord's passion is to be effectual in us, we must imitate what we receive and proclaim to others what we venerate." Again there is the idea of imitation, the following of Christ even in his passion. And this imitation or following must be motivated by love: "If you love, then follow", says Augustine in his homily for Sunday of the fourth week (p. 173).

The fathers of the eastern Church express this idea of imitation in a more forceful and dramatic way. On Saturday of the fifth week we are addressed by St Gregory Nazianzen (*Divine Office* II, p. 247): "Let us accept everything literally, let us imitate the passion by our sufferings, let us reverence the blood by our blood, let us be eager to climb the cross." St Andrew of Crete also urges us to imitate Christ in his passion in the reading for Palm Sunday (p. 255): "Come, then, let us run with him as he presses on to his passion. Let us imitate those who have gone out to meet him, not scattering olive branches or garments or palms in his path, but spreading ourselves before him as best we can, with humility of soul and upright purpose."

Finally, there is that splendid prayer for Palm Sunday:

Almighty, ever-living God,
you gave our Saviour the command
to become man and undergo the cross,
as an example of humility for all men to follow.
We have the lessons of his sufferings;
give us also the fellowship of his resurrection
(*Breviary* version).

The fruits of the passion. The mystery of the cross is a mystery of
love and of unity: "And when I am lifted up from the earth, I
shall draw all men to myself" *(Jn 12:32).* Let us examine this and
other fruits of Christ's saving passion in the light of the Lenten
liturgy.

In the Mass lectionary we meet the theme of reconciliation on
Ash Wednesday, in that great passage from St Paul *(2 Cor
5:20 – 6:2),* in which he urges us to be "reconciled to God".
Reconciliation is surely a key concept of Lent; it underlies our
whole theology of penance. Reconciliation with God is possible
because Christ, by his passion and death, has reconciled us with
the Father. On the fourth Sunday of Lent (Year C) this message
is repeated in the second reading *(2 Cor 5:17-21):*

It is all God's work. It was God who reconciled us with himself through Christ and gave us the work of handing on this
reconciliation. In other words, God in Christ was reconciling the world to himself, not holding men's faults against
them, and he has entrusted to us the news that they are
reconciled.

Reconciliation is a strong term. It implies that there has been
a breakdown in human relations, that some serious rift has
arisen between people as, for example, between married
partners or members of a family or sections of a community. By
becoming reconciled, the former happy relationship is restored.
Something similar occurred between God and his creatures. Sin
brought about a rift in man's relations with God. It produced
division and estrangement, it destroyed the bond of friendship
and intimacy between the two. Christ, the Son of God, came to

53

repair what had been destroyed, to reconcile what had become estranged, to restore peace by his death on the cross.

We know how much Christ longed for unity, unity between the Father and his wayward children, unity among his followers, unity between Jew and Gentile, unity within the whole human family. In his great prayer at the Last Supper, he prayed "That they all may be one", but he knew that he would achieve that unity only by the sacrifice of his life. Caiphas, the high priest, unwittingly prophesied that Christ would die for the people, "and not for the nation only but to gather in unity the scattered children of God" (*Jn 11:52*; see also the gospel for Saturday of the fifth week).

By his life and death Christ atoned for our sins. It is significant that the word atonement derives from the three words "at-one-ment". From whatever angle we consider the saving work of Christ, unity is its ultimate effect; and this unity has its source in God's love. It is all part of God's eternal plan; it is brought about by the saving work of Christ and perfected by the sending of the Holy Spirit at Pentecost.

In the office of readings for Thursday of the fifth week (*Divine Office* II, pp. 231-32), our attention is drawn to the teaching of the Second Vatican Council. In its Constitution on the Church it has this to say:

> God has called together as one all who in faith look upon Jesus as the author of salvation and the source of unity and peace. He has established them as the Church, so that for each and all she may be the visible sacrament of this saving unity.

If our faith is strong, we shall draw from the cross of Christ all its inherent power. The Mass texts for Tuesday of the fifth week illustrate this. Here the image of the "fiery serpent" helps us to understand the healing and redeeming power of the cross. (See first reading, *NB 21:4-9.*) The bronze serpent was placed on a standard, and simply by looking up at it people were healed of their snake bites. For the Church fathers it was a figure of the passion of Christ; it foretold the saving power of the cross. The gospel of that day *(Jn 8:21-30)* perfectly matches this Old Testament reading. In it Jesus, speaking of his own death on the cross, seems to allude to the episode of the bronze serpent. His words are prophetic: "When you have lifted up the Son of Man then you will know that I am he." The cross is a healing power; to look up at Christ with faith is to be saved.

6

INTRODUCING HOLY WEEK

Of all the weeks in the year Holy Week is the one most revered by Christians. It has been hallowed by the events which we commemorate in the liturgy and in a very special way has been consecrated to God. The Church, in celebrating the passion, death and resurrection of Christ, sanctifies and renews herself.

This week was also known in ancient times as "The Great Week", a title which was retained until recently in the old Roman breviary.[1] It is indeed a great week since it constitutes the heart and kernel of the liturgical year. It celebrates the mystery of redemption. The Christians of antiquity had no doubt about its greatness; one early writer summed it up in the revealing phrase: "Easter is the summit."

One of the most penetrating commentaries on Holy Week is that of the German Benedictine nun, Aemiliana Löhr, significantly entitled *The Great Week*.[2] It is full of revealing insights and arresting thoughts, one of which can be of particular help to us in this introductory section. This is that we should enter Holy Week in a spirit of inner peace and recollectedness. We know from experience that these last days before Easter can be a time of frenetic activity; we often get carried away with last-minute preparations for the feast of Easter, and leave the fulfilling of our spiritual obligations to one last great effort.

Aemiliana Löhr, in her first chapter (pp. 12-14), uses the beautiful image of a ship entering port after a long voyage. It is an image of peace: the weeks of effort and strain are over. The Church is like that ship. Lent has been a long voyage, a time of labour and self-discipline, but now in Holy Week the Church has entered port; it is time to rest in the passion of Christ. It may not be easy to take time off for God, but this idea of resting in the passion suggests the attitude of mind we should have in approaching Holy Week.

We could rest in the thought of God's love which is at the origin of all the events we commemorate in this week: "Yes, God loved the world so much that he gave his only Son" *(Jn 3:16)*. The whole passion was motivated by love, the love of God made visible in Christ. Again it is John who tells us: "He had always loved those who were his in the world, but now he showed how perfect his love was" *(Jn 13:1)*.

During Holy Week the Church follows in the footsteps of the Master. The passion narrative comes to life as though it were being re-enacted before our eyes. All the events leading up to the arrest, trial and execution of Jesus are recalled and celebrated. Step by step, scene by scene, we follow along the path which Christ trod during the last days of his mortal life.

The Holy Week liturgy grew out of the devotion of the early Christians[3] in Jerusalem where Jesus endured his passion. Jerusalem, from very early times, became a place of pilgrimage; and pilgrims, then as now, loved to visit the sites of the passion – Gethsemane, the Pretorium, Golgatha, the holy sepulchre. One of the most interesting documents which have come down to us from early times is the travel-diary of the Spanish pilgrim Egeria.[4] It gives us a most graphic account of the Holy Week liturgy as celebrated in Jerusalem about the year 400 A.D.

We have much to learn from the devotion of the ancient Church, as witnessed to in the writings which have survived. It is true that the Christians of Jerusalem had an advantage over us: they were closer to our Lord both in time and place. But our devotion need not be any less. After all, we share in the mysteries of Christ, not through imagination or feeling, though these have their role, but through faith. In the liturgy of Holy Week the Church relives in faith the saving mysteries of the passion, death and resurrection of the Lord.

NOTES

1. *"Majoris Hebdomadae."* Egeria begins her account of Holy Week in Jerusalem with the words: "The next day, Sunday, is the beginning of the

Easter week or, as they call it here, *'The Great Week'.'' Egeria's Travels,* 30, 1.

2. *The Great Week:* An explanation of the liturgy of Holy Week, Longmans, Green, London, 1958.

3. See J. A. Jungmann, SJ "The History of Holy Week as the Heart of the Liturgical Year" in *Studies in Pastoral Liturgy,* ed. Placid Murray, OSB, The Furrow Trust, Maynooth, 1961, pp. 11-24.

4. An excellent English translation with full commentary is now available: *Egeria's Travels,* (ed. John Wilkinson), SPCK, London, 1971.

7

PASSION OR PALM SUNDAY

Passion Sunday, or Palm Sunday as it is more popularly known, inaugurates Holy Week. According to a rubrical note, "On this day the Church celebrates Christ's entrance into Jerusalem to accomplish his paschal mystery." All four evangelists record this event and underline its importance. Jesus is presented as the Messiah-King, entering and taking possession of his city. He comes, however, not as a warrior-king advancing with a great army, but as a humble and gentle Messiah. He fulfils the prophecy of Zechariah *(Zc 9:9)*: "Lo, your king comes to you; triumphant and victorious is he, humble and riding on an ass."

The procession. The procession is characterised by joy, a joy that anticipates that of Easter. It is a procession in honour of Christ the King; that is the reason for the red vestments, the acclamations and hymns in honour of Christ the King. The Church re-enacts the events of the first Palm Sunday: what we read in the gospel comes to life in the procession.[1]

The procession is not just pageantry. It is something very real; in a sense it is even more real than the original event itself, for the Church, in celebrating this event with faith and devotion, is celebrating the mystery hidden within it. The king we acclaim is not just a figure of history, but one who lives and reigns now and forever. The significance of Christ's triumphal entry is perceived only by those who have faith. He enters "to complete his work as our Messiah, to suffer, to die and to rise again".

"Blessed is he who comes in the name of the Lord, hosanna in the highest!" We hear this acclamation at every Mass, at the beginning of the eucharistic prayer. Christ's coming in the eucharistic mystery is a daily happening. In the Palm Sunday procession the Church, represented in each liturgical assembly, goes out to meet and to welcome Christ in a special way.

The procession gives us a kind of preview or foretaste of Easter Sunday. The joy and triumph of Easter breaks through the otherwise sombre liturgy of this day. The palms, which are blessed and carried in procession, are an emblem of victory: "Today we honour Christ our triumphant King by carrying these branches." The resurrection is explicitly mentioned in the responsory sung as the procession enters the Church: "The children of Jerusalem welcomed Christ the King. They proclaimed the resurrection of life."

In the Palm Sunday procession the Church not only commemorates a past event and celebrates a present reality, but also anticipates its final accomplishment. The Church looks forward to the fulfilment of the mystery at the end of time. This eschatological note is sounded in the prayer said at the blessing of the palm branches: "Today we joyfully acclaim Jesus our Messiah and King. May we reach one day the happiness of the new and everlasting Jerusalem." One of the petitions for the morning office, addressed to Christ, also has this note of longing for future fulfilment: "You went to Jerusalem to endure the passion and enter into glory; lead your Church into the paschal feast of eternal life."

Liturgy of the Word. The day is called both Palm Sunday and Passion Sunday: the palm for victory and the passion for suffering. The procession heralds the victory of Easter Sunday; in contrast to this, the Liturgy of the Word which follows plunges us into the atmosphere of Good Friday. Christ will indeed conquer, but it will be through his passion and death.[2]

The first reading is from the prophet Isaiah *(50:4-7).* The prophet's sufferings at the hands of his enemies prefigure those of Christ. His calm acceptance of insult and injury makes us think of Christ's humility under even greater provocation. It is suffering freely accepted and willingly endured. We meet this idea of voluntary acceptance again in the second reading *(Ph 2:6-11),* where we are told: "He (Christ) was humbler yet, even to accepting death, death on a cross." It is also the theme of the preface: "Though he was sinless, he suffered willingly for sinners; though innocent, he accepted death to save the guilty."

The second reading gives us a profound insight into the mystery of redemption, St Paul, addressing the Philippians, speaks of the self-emptying *(kenosis)* of Christ. He not only "emptied himself to assume the conditon of a slave" but humbled himself even to accepting death on a cross. This was the ultimate in humility and abasement, to become an outcast, one rejected by society. But St Paul, having sounded the depths of Christ's sufferings, immediately directs our thoughts upwards: "But God raised him high and gave him the name which is above all other names."

The solemn reading of the passion narrative is the most characteristic feature of the Mass. According to the three-year cycle, the gospel account is that of Matthew, Mark or Luke. Traditionally, it is the passion according to St Matthew which is read this day.

The reading of the gospel is stripped of the usual ceremonial, even at a high Mass: no lights, or incense, even the sign of the cross is omitted at the beginning. It begins with the bare announcement: "The passion of our Lord Jesus Christ according to Matthew". The gospel of the passion needs no adornment; it does not even require an introduction or homily; it speaks for itself. When read with reverence it cannot fail to make a deep impression.

There are many books on the life of Christ, many meditations and tracts on the passion. Nothing makes a greater impact on us, however, than the sober but poignant accounts of the Lord's passion given us by the evangelists themselves. Here no attempt is made to play on our feelings or to present a highly coloured account of what happened. Neither do we detect any playing down of the suffering, physical and moral, endured by our Lord. It is a story simply told, with dignity and restraint. And yet it tells all, so much so that we may well imagine that we are witnessing these events. There is drama and pathos but also serenity. The figure of Christ towers above his accusers and persecutors.

The custom of employing three readers for the gospel is a

63

good one. This helps to sustain attention and interest. It also highlights the words of Christ, a role fittingly played by the celebrant himself. A second reader will act as a narrator and a third will assume the other parts.

NOTES

1. The procession had its origin in Jerusalem (4th century) where it took place on Sunday evening. The people assembled on The Mount of Olives and from there went in procession into the city. They carried olive branches and were accompanied by the bishop who represented Christ. See *Egeria's Travels,* (ed. John Wilkinson), pp. 132-33.
2. The procession was introduced to the Roman liturgy at a comparatively late date, a fact which helps explain the remarkable contrast between the processional texts and those of the Mass. For history of Palm Sunday, see N. Maurice-Denis, ''Le dimanche des Rameaux'' in *La Maison-Dieu* 41, 1955, pp. 16-33; and A. Chavasse in *L'Eglise en Prière,* (ed. A. G. Martimort), Desclée, Tournai, 1965, pp. 730-32.

8

MONDAY TO WEDNESDAY

No special celebrations mark the first half of Holy Week. During these days the Church ponders deeply on the mystery of the Lord's passion, as witness the texts of the missal, lectionary and breviary. To read and reflect on these texts is to acquire the authentic spirit of Holy Week. It is to "rest in the passion of Christ".

In the office of readings the Letter to the Hebrews, begun on Sunday of the fifth week, continues to be read. This reveals the deep significance and redemptive value of Christ's sufferings. Here Christ is presented in his dual role of priest and victim. The efficacy of his sacrifice is declared unequivocally: "By virtue of that one single offering, he has achieved the eternal perfection of all whom he is sanctifying" *(Heb 10:13)*.

The theme of the "imitation of Christ", already commented on in the Lenten liturgy, recurs here. It finds expression in the patristic readings of the morning office. What Christ endured for our sakes is shown as the pattern of Christian living. Thus St Basil, in the reading for Tuesday, has this to say:

> So, for perfection of life it is necessary not only to imitate Christ, in the examples of gentleness, and humility, and patience which he gave us in his life, but also to imitate him in his death, as Paul the imitator of Christ says: "Becoming like him in his death, that if possible I may attain the resurrection from the dead" *(Divine Office* II, p. 270).

St Augustine also broaches this theme of imitation in his homily on the fullness of Christian love as exemplified by Christ when he laid down his life for us. We must imitate his example, and like the martyrs, be ready to lay down our lives for our brethren. St Augustine concludes: "So let us love one another as Christ loved us and gave himself for us."

On Spy Wednesday, as it is called, the betrayal by Judas is introduced. The gospel *(Mt 26:14-25)* describes how Judas went to the chief priests and offered to betray Jesus for thirty pieces of silver. With this act of treachery on the part of a trusted disciple of the Lord the hour of darkness is at hand.

9

HOLY THURSDAY

Holy Thursday stands at the cross roads between Lent and Easter. It is the last day of Lent and its evening Mass ushers in the paschal triduum. It is the final preparation for Easter and already initiates the Easter celebration.

Preparation is the key word for this day. Everything is made in readiness for the pasch. So it was with the first Holy Thursday when the Lord sent Peter and John to make preparations: "Go and make the preparations for us to eat the passover" *(Lk 22:8).*

For the faithful it is a day of spiritual preparation. In ancient times the public penitents were reconciled with the Church on this day; in a solemn and public rite they were received back into full communion with the Church; absolved from their sins, they could now celebrate the pasch and receive their paschal communion with the rest of the faithful. It would be in line with Christian tradition to make our Easter confession on this day, if we have not already done so.

Two Masses are celebrated on this day, one in the cathedral churches only (the Chrism Mass) and the other (Evening Mass of the Lord's Supper) in parish churches and churches of religious orders. The Chrism Mass includes the blessing of the oils needed for baptism and other sacraments. Here the emphasis is on the theme of priesthood and its institution by Christ. The evening Mass commemorates more specifically the institution of the Eucharist. The two themes are intimately connected, but it helps us to distinguish them by having two celebrations.

The Chrism Mass. As mentioned above the Chrism Mass is celebrated only in cathedral churches. It takes place in the morning, the diocesan bishop acting as consecrator of the oils and as chief concelebrant. It is an impressive and beautiful rite and is catechetically very rich.

In this coming together of the people of God we have a very expressive manifestation of the Church, for the diocese is the Church of God in miniature. In ancient times it was possible for a bishop to celebrate the Eucharist surrounded by almost his entire flock. This is hardly feasible today, yet it remains the ideal. This ideal is well expressed in the Liturgy Constitution of Vatican II:

> They (the faithful) must be convinced that the pre-eminent manifestation of the Church consists in the full, active participation of all God's holy people in these liturgical celebrations, especially in the same Eucharist, in a single prayer, at one altar, at which the bishop presides surrounded by his college of priests and ministers (41).

The Holy Thursday liturgy in the cathedral comes very close to this ideal. Here we have the bishop, head of the local Church, surrounded by priests from all the parishes of his diocese and by priests representing the religious orders. The bishop concelebrates Mass with his priests as a sign of unity and fellowship. He is assisted by them in the blessing of the oils. The deacons and other ministers are also present and take an active part.

As a visible expression of the hierarchical Church this occasion is almost unique. It is all the more so if the faithful of the diocese are there in large numbers. Their presence and participation is greatly desired, for the Church is incomplete if it does not include the lay people of God. Those of the faithful who attend may receive communion at the Chrism Mass and again in the evening.

It is significant that the oils for use in the sacraments are blessed within the context of the Eucharist and in close proximity to Easter. This is not by accident. The sacraments derive their meaning and efficacy from the paschal mystery of Christ. This mystery is renewed in each eucharistic celebration and with special solemnity in the paschal feast. To quote again from the Liturgy Constitution:

68

Thus for well-disposed members of the faithful, the liturgy of the sacraments and the sacramentals sanctifies almost every event of their lives with the divine grace which flows from the paschal mystery of the passion, death and resurrection of Christ. From this source all sacraments and sacramentals draw their power (61).

All the sacraments have a connection with Easter; they are *paschal* sacraments. We might remind ourselves of this when we assist at a baptism, confirmation or ordination and the holy oil of chrism is used; or when someone is anointed with the oil of the sick.

The priesthood is the major theme of the Chrism Mass. In bequeathing the mystery of the Eucharist to the Church, Christ also instituted the Christian priesthood. The texts of the Mass present a catechesis of the priesthood, referring not only to the ministerial priesthood but also to the general priesthood of the faithful. Thus in the entrance antiphon the assembly acclaims: "Jesus Christ has made us a kingdom of priests to serve his God and Father." This is repeated in the second reading and is echoed in the preface.

All priesthood is a sharing in the one priesthood of Christ. He is our Mediator and High Priest. His anointing is from the Holy Spirit. This is brought out in the reading from Isaiah *(61:1-3, 6, 8-9)* and in the gospel from Luke *(4:16-21)*, in which our Lord quotes and applies to himself the prophetic texts: "The spirit of the Lord has been given to me, for he has anointed me."

Through the sacrament of holy orders men share in a unique way in the priesthood of Christ: to them alone is given the power to remit sins and to change bread and wine into the body and blood of Christ; they do this in the name and through the power of Christ. They are in a special way pastors and teachers of the Church, as well as administrators of the sacraments. All this is summed up in the preface:

He appoints them to renew in his name the sacrifice of our redemption as they set before your family his paschal meal. He calls them to lead your holy people in love, nourish

69

them by your word, and strengthen them through the sacraments.

It is not easy for the priest to live up to the demands of his vocation and ministry. He needs the prayer and support of his fellow Christians. He needs from time to time to ''fan into the flame'' the gift that God gave him *(2 Tm 1:6)*.

One of the most impressive features of the Chrism Mass, and a recent addition, is the renewal of commitment to priestly service. After the gospel and homily, the bishop invites his priests to renew their dedication to Christ and his Church. Together they solemnly undertake to unite themselves more closely to Christ, to be his faithful ministers, to teach and to offer the holy sacrifice in his name, to lead and guide others to him.

In this act of commitment the bishop asks for himself the prayers of all his people. He needs their prayers. As that great bishop, St Augustine, once said to his people: ''While I am frightened by what I am to you, I am also consoled by what I share with you. For you I am a bishop, with you I am a Christian.''[1]

In a very real way a bishop represents Christ in his diocese: ''The bishop is to be considered as the High Priest of his flock, from whom the life in Christ of his faithful is in some way derived and upon whom it in some way depends'' (Liturgy Constitution, 41).

The blessing of the oils and consecration of the chrism may take place after the renewal of commitment or at a later point in the Mass. The older tradition places the blessing of the oil of the sick just before the end of the eucharistic prayer; the blessing of the oil of catechumens and the consecration of the chrism is of special interest. All the concelebrating priests associate themselves with the consecratory prayer, which is one of the most solemn in the liturgy. It provides an effective lesson on the dignity and power of the sacraments, especially the sacrament of baptism.

The Easter triduum begins with the Evening Mass of the Lord's Supper.

NOTES

1. *The Divine Office* III, p. 274*, for the feast of St Januarius, office of readings.
2. *Constitution on the Sacred Liturgy* of the Second Vatican Council, II, no. 47, trans. J. Rogers in *Liturgy — Renewal and Adaptation,* (ed. A. Flannery, OP), Scepter, Dublin, 1968.
3. *Egeria's Travels,* (ed. John Wilkinson), SPCK, 1971, pp. 134-35; see commentary pp. 74-75.
4. See N. Lazure, "Le lavement des pieds" in *Jeudi Saint* vol. 20, series *Assemblées du Seigneur,* Cerf, Paris, 1973, pp. 53-64.
5. Encyclical *Mysterium Fidei,* no. 63.

10

THE EASTER TRIDUUM

The word triduum in Catholic devotional practice suggests the idea of preparation. We may, for example, prepare for the feast of a saint by observing three days of prayer in the saint's honour; or we may seek to obtain some special favour by holding a triduum of prayer and intercession.

The Easter or paschal triduum was seen as a three-days' preparation for the feast of Easter. It comprised Thursday, Friday and Saturday of Holy Week. It was a triduum of the passion.

In the new Calendar and reformed Order of Holy Week, a shift of emphasis has taken place. The triduum is presented not just as a period of preparation but as a unified whole. It is a triduum of the passion and resurrection; it embraces the whole celebration of the paschal mystery. This is what the Calendar says:

> Christ redeemed mankind and gave perfect glory to God principally through his paschal mystery: by dying he destroyed our death and by rising he restored our life. The Easter triduum of the passion and resurrection of Christ is thus the culmination of the entire liturgical year.

It then goes on to determine the exact duration of the triduum:

> The Easter triduum begins with the evening Mass of the Lord's supper, reaches its high point in the Easter Vigil and closes with Vespers on Easter Sunday.

This unifying of the Easter celebration is closer to the spirit of the New Testament and of early Christian tradition. Christ himself, in alluding to his passion and death, did not dissociate these from his resurrection. In the gospel for Wednesday of the second week of Lent *(Mt 20:17-28)* he speaks of them conjointly: "They will condemn him to death and will hand him over to the pagans to be mocked and scourged and crucified; and on the third day he will rise again."

It is significant that among the Church fathers both St Ambrose and St Augustine conceive the Easter triduum as a unity embracing both the suffering and glorification of Jesus. Thus the Bishop of Milan, in one of his writings, refers to the three holy days *(triduum illud sacrum)* as the three days "within which he suffered, lay in the tomb, and arose, the three days of which he said: 'Destroy this temple and in three days I will raise it up'".[1] St Augustine, in one of his letters, refers to "the three most sacred days of his (Christ's) crucifixion, burial and resurrection".[2]

These three days, beginning with the evening Mass on Holy Thursday and concluding with evening prayer on Easter Sunday, form a unity and should be viewed as such. It follows that Easter, the Christian pasch, consists essentially of a three-day celebration; it embraces both the dark and radiant sides of Christ's saving mystery. Spread over these three days are the different phases of the Easter mystery. The Easter triduum may be likened to a triptych: three pictures, each depicting a part of the scene, together forming a unity; each picture is complete but needs to be viewed in relation to the other two.

Of interest in this connection is the fact that Good Friday and Holy Saturday do not officially belong to the season of Lent. According to the new Calendar, Lent begins on Ash Wednesday and is concluded on Holy Thursday, exclusive of the Mass of the Lord's Supper.[3] Friday and Saturday of Holy Week are not the last two days of Lent, but the first two days of "the most sacred triduum".

Thoughts for the triduum. The unity of the paschal mystery has something important to teach us. It teaches us that sorrow is not simply followed by joy, but that it already contains joy. Jesus

74

used many images to express this; for instance, at the Last Supper he told his apostles: "You will be sorrowful, but your sorrow will turn to joy" *(Jn 16:20)*. It is as though sorrow were one of the ingredients from which joy would be fashioned. The image of a woman in the pains of childbirth beautifully expresses this. Her pain actually generates joy, the joy "that a man has been born into the world".

Other images also come to mind. The whole cycle of nature speaks of life out of death: "Unless a wheat grain falls on the ground and dies, it remains only a single grain; but if it dies, it yields a rich harvest" *(Jn 12:24)*.

Easter is our passover; it is a passing over from death to life, from darkness to light, from fast to feast. Our Lord said: "But when you fast, put oil on your head and wash your face" *(Mt 6:17)*. The fast is the beginning of the feast.

Suffering is not a good thing in itself and so is not to be sought after for its own sake. The Christian approach to it is positive and realistic. In the life of Christ, and above all in the cross, we see its redemptive value. The crucifix can never be just a painful reminder of what Christ suffered for us. It is an object in which we can glory because it is transfigured by the glory of the resurrection.

In our own lives joy and sorrow intermingle. To shrink from pain and sorrow at all costs and to seek joy and pleasure for their own sakes are both mistaken attitudes. The Christian way is the way illuminated by the teaching and example of Christ. It is the way of the cross which is also the way of the resurrection; it is self-forgetfulness, it is losing oneself for Christ's sake, it is life out of death. The paschal mystery, which we celebrate during these days of the triduum, is the pattern and the programme our own lives should follow.

NOTES

1. Letter 36, published in *Saint Ambrose — Letters,* trans. M. M. Beyenka in *The Fathers of the Church* series, Catholic University of America, Washington, 1967, p. 194.

11

EVENING MASS OF THE LORD'S SUPPER

The evening Mass commemorates the Last Supper and the institution of the Eucharist. Everything seems to evoke the memory of that paschal meal which Christ shared with his disciples: the time (late evening), the recalling in the readings of the institution of the Eucharist, Christ's final discourse and the washing of the disciples' feet; the insertion into the eucharistic prayer of the words: "The day before he suffered to save us and all men, that is today, he took bread in his sacred hands. . . ."

It was in the course of this meal that our Lord founded his own memorial, the Eucharist:

> At the Last Supper, on the night he was betrayed, our Saviour instituted the eucharistic sacrifice of his body and blood. This he did in order to perpetuate the sacrifice of the Cross throughout the ages until he should come again, and so to entrust to his beloved spouse, the Church, a memorial of his death and resurrection: a sacrament of love, a sign of unity, a bond of charity, a paschal banquet in which Christ is consumed, the mind is filled with grace, and a pledge of future glory is given to us.

"A sacrament of love, a sign of unity, a bond of charity" — that is what the Eucharist was intended to be; and on this evening it reveals itself very clearly in that light. What could be more expressive of unity than a meal shared among a family or among friends? The Eucharist is a meal, Christ is our host, the altar a table and we are God's family. The Mass is not only a sacred meal, but that is the aspect of the eucharistic mystery which is highlighted this evening. It is under the symbolism of a sacred meal that we discover the community dimension of the Mass.

A spirit of joy characterises the Mass. It is a deep, interior joy; it is the joy which Christ experienced in his own soul on this occasion. He had looked forward to it: "I have longed and longed to share this paschal meal with you." In that final discourse, recorded by John *(13-17)*, the word joy occurs very frequently. For every Jewish family the passover meal was a time of great family joy; it was an event eagerly awaited. Christ would have experienced this joy, but his joy went much deeper. His was the joy of total sacrifice, the joy of one who gives without counting the cost. Christ rejoices in the fulfilment of his Father's will of which he is the perfect human instrument.

This joy is given liturgical expression in the Mass. The chants are joyful, the *Gloria* is sung or recited (in some places to the accompaniment of bells), and white vestments are worn. Everything suggests joy and festivity. Only the *Alleluia* is absent. This is to remind us that it is not yet Easter Sunday.

The entrance antiphon sounds a triumphal note: "It is our duty to glory in the cross of our Lord Jesus Christ. He saves us and sets us free; through him we find salvation, life and resurrection." It is very impressive when this is sung as celebrant and ministers approach the altar preceded by the processional cross, the emblem of victory.

The Eucharist is Christ's own memorial of his sacrifice on the cross. There is an intimate and necessary connection between the Mass and Calvary. What our Lord does at the Last Supper, and commands his disciples to do in memory of him, announces and anticipates his self-oblation on Good Friday. It is significant that in Jerusalem on this day the holy sacrifice was offered "behind the cross", that is at Golgatha.

The opening prayer declares that Christ gave us this sacrament to reveal his love, and goes on to ask that in it we may find the fullness of love and life.

The first reading *(Ex 12:1-8, 11-14)* gives the Old Testament instructions concerning the passover meal. It prefigures the passover of Christ and the paschal banquet which he will institute. By instituting the Eucharist and undergoing his passion in the course of the paschal celebrations, Christ intended to show that he was the fulfilment of the Old Testament figures, that he was the true lamb, slain in sacrifice, whose blood would save his people. In the course of the paschal meal he changed bread and wine into his body and blood, thus establishing the paschal rite of the Church.

The second reading *(1 Cor 11:23-26)* gives us St Paul's account of the Last Supper and the institution of the Eucharist. It is clear that at the time he was writing (about 57 A.D.) the liturgical tradition was firmly established. As this may be the earliest account of the institution it is of particular interest and value. It witnesses to the faith of the primitive Church in the Real Presence, the sacrificial character of the Eucharist ("This is my body, which is for you") and its awareness that in celebrating the Eucharist it is fulfilling the Lord's command: "Do this as a memorial of me." It also shows that the Eucharist is both memorial and promise, that it not only constitutes Christ's memorial *(anamnesis)* but also heralds his return at the end of time.

The gospel *(Jn 13:1-15)* describes the washing of the disciples' feet. It is well chosen to illustrate the theme of fraternal love. The Eucharist is the sacrament of love: it commits us to a life of love and service. Christ taught the doctrine of love by his whole life. At the Last Supper he repeats and develops his teaching, and reinforces his words by symbolic action. The gesture of the washing of the feet puzzled and astonished the apostles; but, in a way that no words could, it drove home the lesson of mutual love and service: "I have given you an example so that you may copy what I have done to you."

The liturgy has preserved for optional use the medieval rite of the washing of feet. After the gospel and homily the celebrant puts on an apron and takes a towel. Twelve men, representing the apostles, come forward and take their places in front of the sanctuary. The priest goes to each man, pours water over his feet and dries them. As the gospel scene is thus re-enacted the choir may sing some of the traditional antiphons, made up of sentences from St John, such as: "I give you a new commandment: love one another as I have loved you." This miming of the gospel is a kind of audio-visual aid. It may strike us as rather strange but in

79

the time of our Lord there was nothing strange about washing the feet of guests; it was a simple gesture of hospitality. Performed by Christ at the Last Supper it had a much deeper significance. It conveyed, first of all, the message of mutual service; authority must be understood and practised as a form of service. Here Christ has given the perfect example. At a deeper level, Christ in this gesture is prophesying his own death. The washing of the disciples' feet symbolised the supreme act of loving service for mankind, Christ's atoning sacrifice. Its message is that not only should we imitate Christ's spirit of service in little things, but be prepared to follow him all the way even, if necessary, to the extent of laying down our lives.

The Liturgy of the Eucharist now begins. At the presentation of gifts (Offertory) the idea of service, in this case service of the poor, is again to the fore. It is customary at this Mass to have a collection for the poor; and at this point of the celebration, gifts for the poor, in money or in kind, are brought in procession to the altar together with the bread and wine. During the procession an appropriate hymn is sung. The traditional hymn of fraternal love *Ubi caritas et amor, Deus ibi est* (Where charity and love are found, there is God) is very appropriate.

The preface is that of the Holy Eucharist. If eucharistic Prayer I is employed, as seems appropriate, the ancient text is suitably adapted to fit this particular occasion: "Father, accept this offering from your whole family in memory of the day when Jesus Christ, our Lord, gave the mysteries of his body and blood for his disciples to celebrate."

At communion time an extraordinary impression of unity is created. There are no private Masses and only one eucharistic celebration in each church apart from cathedrals. The local community, young and old, priests and laity, gather round a single altar, and the clergy of the parish or religious community concelebrate or simply receive communion. In this way the unity of the Church, the body of Christ, is highlighted: a unity strengthened and sustained by the Eucharist, the sacrament of love.

After the distribution of communion, the ciborium with hosts for Good Friday is left on the altar, and Mass concludes with the prayer after communion. After Mass the priest, accompanied by his ministers, carries the blessed sacrament in procession to the altar of repose. This solemn procession with lights and incense and the singing of the *Pange lingua* evokes the feast of the Body and Blood of Christ. It brings out another dimension of the Eucharist, that of permanent sacrament. In the words of Pope Paul VI: "It is not only while the sacrifice is being offered and the sacrament is being constituted that Christ is truly Emmanuel, 'God with us'; for day and night he is in our midst, dwelling among us full of grace and truth."

The Holy Thursday liturgy is over, but not personal prayer and devotion. The faithful are encouraged to continue adoration at the altar of repose for a suitable time between now and midnight. This is a kind of private vigil which commemorates Christ's own vigil in the garden of Gethsemane when he was overcome with sorrow. We are reminded of our Lord's words to the three disciples: "Wait here and keep awake with me" and "So you had not the strength to keep awake with me one hour" *(Mt 26:38-41)*.

12

GOOD FRIDAY

Good Friday is a day of intense sorrow, but of sorrow sweetened by Christian hope. The remembrance of what Christ suffered for us cannot fail to arouse in us feelings of sorrow and compassion, and of regret for our share in the sins of the world.

Devotion to the passion of Christ is deep-rooted in Christian piety. It is witnessed to in the early Church and, indeed, in the New Testament writings. The pilgrim, Egeria, describing the Good Friday ceremonies in Jerusalem in 400 A.D., has left us a vivid and moving account of the people's reaction to the passion readings: ''It is impressive to see the way the people are moved by these readings, and how they mourn. You could hardly believe how every single one of them weeps during these three hours, old and young alike, because of the manner in which the Lord suffered for us.''[1]

The Good Friday liturgy presents a synthesis of all that is best in devotion to the passion of Christ. The spirit of the early Church is there with its emphasis on the glory of the cross; also the realism, tenderness and compassion of the Middle Ages. The insights of every age, the piety of both western and eastern Christianity are somehow blended together to form one harmonious whole.

Celebration of the Lord's passion. Celebration of the Lord's passion takes place in the afternoon, about three o'clock, the time when Jesus was crucified. As a general rule only one celebration is allowed in each church. In Ireland, because of the very large numbers who throng the churches on this day, a second celebration is allowed.[2]

83

The celebration falls into three parts: Liturgy of the Word; veneration of the cross; holy communion.

Liturgy of the Word. The ceremony begins in a very simple way. The celebrant and ministers approach the altar in silence. There they make a reverence or, according to the ancient manner, prostrate themselves. All pray in silence for a little while. The priest then reads the opening prayer after which all sit down to listen to the readings.

The first reading *(Isaiah 52:13 – 53:12)* presents us with the "suffering servant", a prophetic figure in whom Christian tradition, and the New Testament itself, has recognised Christ.[3] Christ in his passion is indeed the "man of sorrows" so powerfully portrayed in this poem. It is all there: his sufferings and humiliations, his rejection by his people, his atoning death; even the details of the passion narrative are there, e.g. "He was pierced through for our faults."

This passage sets the tone for the Good Friday service. Yet even here the darkness is shot through with light and hope. The very first line of the poem points to ultimate victory: "See, my servant will prosper, he shall be lifted up, exalted, rise to great heights." It is with this note of exaltation that the poem is concluded. Because God's servant accepts his role of expiatory victim, he brings peace, healing and justification to many: "His soul's anguish over, he shall see the light and be content. By his sufferings shall my servant justify many, taking their faults on himself."

The second reading *(Heb 4:14-16; 5:7-9)* presents Christ in his priestly role, reconciling men to God through the sacrifice of his own life.[4] He is both priest and victim, offerer and offered; he is our mediator with the Father. In this reading we contemplate Christ in his heavenly existence and in his present activity. In the gospel we have the record of his suffering and death.

Christ is not a figure of the past, nor is he a remote, impassive personage. He has experienced our human lot in every way, sin excepted. He can therefore sympathise with us in our sorrow and wretchedness, because he too has suffered in his sacred humanity.

The Gospel. "The passion of our Lord Jesus Christ according to John." With this simple introduction the reader begins the Good Friday gospel *(Jn 18:1 – 19:42).* It seems to have always been the tradition of the Roman Church that it is the passion narrative of St John that is read on this day. St John, the theologian and mystic, views the passion of Jesus more profoundly than the other evangelists, in the light of the Resurrection. His Easter faith transfigures each detail and episode of this last phase of our Lord's earthly life.[5]

Take, for example, the treatment of the cross in St John. In itself it is something cruel and barbarous; but since Christ redeemed mankind by the wood of the cross it is an object of veneration. It is more than that. For St John the cross is a kind of throne. The raising of Jesus on the cross is described as an "exaltation", a term which suggests at once the idea of being lifted up and glorified. It is St John who tells us that Jesus bore his own cross.

The sufferings of our Lord are not minimised, and yet an atmosphere of peace and serenity pervades the whole account. It is Christ, not his persecutors, who is in control of the situation. There is no constraint: he freely goes to his execution; with perfect liberty and complete awareness of the significance of the events, he goes to meet his fate. The motive, the ultimate explanation, is love. The cross is the supreme revelation of the love of God.

In the portrait given by St John, Jesus appears in a three-fold role: as king, judge and saviour. The mockery of the soldiers and the crowning with thorns only serve to underline his kingship. In the very act of condemning him it is Jesus, not Pilate, who is shown as judge; before his words and before his cross we stand condemned or justified. Finally, as saviour, Jesus gathers his people in unity around his cross. The Church, represented by the seamless robe, is formed. On Mary, his mother, is conferred a spiritual maternity: she becomes mother of all the living. From the cross Jesus renders up his spirit, thus inaugurating the final period of salvation. From his pierced side flow blood and water, symbols of salvation and of the life-giving Spirit. Christ is shown as the true paschal lamb, whose blood of old saved the Israelites.

To look on him with faith is to be saved.

General intercessions. In the general intercessions we have a survival of an ancient form of the prayer of the faithful. At one time such solemn prayers of intercession appears to have been a common feature of the Roman liturgy.[6] In this extended and elaborate form they are retained only on this one day in the year. In the ten great prayers of intercession the Church looks out on the whole world and earnestly pleads on behalf of all mankind.

This prayer is truly universal; it includes all categories of people. It is fitting that it should be so on this day when Christian people everywhere are gathered round the cross of Christ, associating themselves with his priestly prayer. His prayer extended to all because his love included all. "For our sake he opened his arms on the cross" in a gesture which embraced the whole world. The cross on which he died is, in Christian tradition, a symbol of universality: its four corners point to the four corners of the world.

These ancient Good Friday prayers have been adapted to present day circumstances. They reflect the ecumenical spirit of our day. There is no mention now of heretics and schismatics but of "all our brothers and sisters who share our faith in Jesus Christ". That wider ecumenism which seeks closer ties of friendship with non-Christian religions is not lacking either. In the prayer for the Jewish people, for example, there is respect and love. They are referred to as "the first to hear the word of God", and we ask that they may grow in the love of God's name and in faithfulness to his covenant.

Two new prayers, very relevant to our time, have been added: "for those who do not believe in Christ", and "for those who do not believe in God". It is salutary to remember that Christians form only a small minority of the world's population: by comparison with the millions of non-Christians the Church of Christ is indeed "a little flock". The harvest is therefore very great, and we should pray "for those who do not believe in Christ, that the light of the Holy Spirit may show them the way to salvation".

The other prayer is for those who do not believe in God.

86

Atheism is widespread today; science, technology, a materialistic philosophy and other factors have had an undermining effect on religious belief. In great areas of the world people live under regimes which are militantly anti-religious. There are parts of the world where the light of the Gospel can scarcely penetrate. But all, whether Christian or atheist, form part of the one human family. We pray for all our brothers and sisters outside the fold, that by living sincere and upright lives they may come to the knowledge of God.

Last of all, there is a prayer for those in special need: the sick, the dying, travellers, prisoners, etc. These general intercessions are truly universal. In this great exercise of intercession, in which all the faithful are actively engaged, the Church is most surely recognised in her role of *ecclesia orans*, "the praying Church".

The veneration of the cross. The eucharistic sacrifice is not offered on Good Friday. The central part of the Mass, the eucharistic prayer, is missing. In its place we have the moving ceremony of the veneration of the cross. This is followed by a simple communion service.

The very absence of the eucharistic sacrifice this day brings home to us the intimate relationship between the sacrifice of Calvary and the Mass. Christ died once-for-all for our sins. His sacrifice is unique and all sufficient. But the memorial of that death and sacrifice is celebrated at every Mass. In each celebration of the Eucharist "the work of our redemption is renewed". On this day the Church's gaze is fixed on Calvary itself where Christ offered his life in atonement for our sins.

The rite of veneration has two forms. The celebrant will choose the form which he considers more suitable. The first form consists of a gradual unveiling of the cross. Standing at the altar, the priest uncovers the upper part of the cross, unveils it and says or sings: "This is the wood of the cross", to which the people reply: "Come, let us worship." They then kneel down and venerate the cross in silence. There follows a second unveiling, that of the right arm of the cross, and again the invitation to worship. Finally the priest uncovers the entire cross and there is a third veneration.

Although this first form has a long and interesting history, the second form seems more effective. Here there is a solemn procession with the unveiled cross from the church door to the sanctuary. The cross is carried by the priest or deacon accompanied by ministers with lighted candles. On the way to the altar there are three "stations" during which the cross is venerated. Near the entrance, in the middle of the church and at the entrance to the sanctuary, the priest or deacon carrying the cross stops, lifts it up and says or sings: "This is the wood of the cross"; the response and act of veneration follow as above. The cross is now placed in position at the entrance to the sanctuary so that all the faithful may approach to venerate it either by a genuflection or by kissing it.

Ideally everyone in the congregation should be given the opportunity to pay personal homage to the crucified Saviour. In the simple gesture of kissing the cross, popular piety expresses itself spontaneously and movingly. To the sombre and majestic liturgy of this day, it introduces a personal and tender note. The gesture of kissing the cross also has a long history behind it: the Christians of Jerusalem venerated it in this way on Good Friday as early as the fourth century.[7]

As the faithful approach to kiss the cross, antiphons, hymns and other appropriate compositions are sung or recited. Some of these are of great antiquity, and even in translation they impress us by their beauty and depth.

The first antiphon surprises us by its joyful character: "We worship you, Lord, we venerate your cross, we praise your resurrection. Through your cross you brought joy to the world." If the cross is never absent from the Christian life, neither is joy. Even on Good Friday we could meditate on the joy of Christ, the joy of total sacrifice.

Next come the famous *Improperia* or "Reproaches", so called because in these verses Christ reproaches his people for their ingratitude. He recounts all his favours on their behalf: he led them out of Egypt, brought them safely through the desert, fed them with manna, worked all sorts of wonders for them; in return for all these favours they treated him with contempt. Antithesis such as: "I led you out of Egypt from slavery to freedom, but you led your Saviour to the cross'', is used to effect throughout the whole composition. Interspersed between the reproaches we have the poignant refrain: ''My people, what have I done to you? How have I offended you? Answer me!'', and then the *Trisagion:* ''Holy is God! Holy and strong! Holy immortal One, have mercy on us!''

Christ reproaches all of us, not only those who crucify him. But he does so in a gentle way which arouses our compassion rather than feelings of guilt. It is our ingratitude and hardness of heart that are questioned. The only response to these questions and reproaches is the silent one of kissing the feet of the crucified Lord.

These *Improperia* combine religious sentiment with theological perception. For the Christ, who appeals to his people, is the pre-existent Word. As Word of God, he was present and at work throughout all the stages of sacred history; he guided the chosen people, he shaped the course of their history. He is the Word Incarnate; and while the memory of his sufferings elicits our compassion, we may not for a moment forget that he is the All Holy One.

The faithful continue to file up to the cross, and now the choir begins the hymn *Pange lingua.* This hymn[8] has been likened to a victory march. It recounts the glorious victory which Christ won over his adversary Satan. Then in one strophe it evokes the scene of the crucifixion in all its cruel reality; but even here the redemptive value of these sufferings is not lost sight of. Then in a note of great tenderness the poet addresses the cross itself, begging it to relax its rigour. Here we have a splendid blending of ancient and medieval devotion to the cross and passion.

The glory of the cross. That great pontiff and father of the Church, Pope St Leo, has left us in his sermons many beautiful and arresting thoughts on the passion and cross of the Lord, which may help our Good Friday meditations.[9]

In Sermon 55 he says that ''Christ's passion contains the mystery of our salvation''; that it is for us ''the stepping-stone to glory'' and that it symbolises ''the true altar of prophecy''.

On Tuesday of the fifth week of Lent, in the office of readings

(*Divine Office* II, pp. 217-19), we have one of his finest sermons on the passion. In it he refers to "the glory of the cross which shines on heaven and earth". Then there is that unforgettable passage:

> O wonderful power of the cross! O indescribable glory of the passion! There is the tribunal of the Lord, and the judgement of the world, and the power of the crucified one.

The cross is "the source of all blessings, the cause of all graces".

In a sermon preached on Passion Sunday, he could even speak of "the feast of the Lord's passion" (*festivitas dominicae passionis*). This may sound like a contradiction in terms but not if we view the work of redemption as a unified whole, as the fathers of the Church did. Viewed with the eyes of faith, contemplated in the light of Christ's Easter victory, the cross is indeed "the trophy of his triumph" and "the adorable sign of salvation". For that reason the joy of Easter does not obliterate the memory of the passion and Calvary; in fact, in the time of Pope St Leo the gospel reading for Easter included the account of the passion together with that of the resurrection of the Lord.[10]

The communion rite. The altar is now covered with a cloth and the corporal and book are placed on it. The ciborium, containing the hosts consecrated at last evening's Mass, is brought to the altar. Two ministers with lighted candles accompany the priest or deacon, and place their candles on or near the altar.

The usual Mass prayers of preparation for the reception of the sacrament follow: the Lord's Prayer with its embolism and acclamation and the priest's private prayer of preparation; then the showing of the Host with the words, "This is the Lamb of God", and the response, "Lord, I am not worthy".

What is the special significance of our communion this day? In answer to this question we may cite St Paul who alludes to a deep and mysterious relationship between sacramental communion and the passion and death of Christ. In his instructions on the Lord's Supper he reminds the Corinthians: "Until the Lord comes, therefore, every time you eat this bread and drink this cup, you are proclaiming his death" *(1 Cor 11:25-26).*

But the Eucharist is not only a proclamation, it is also a participation in the death of Christ. It is a communion with the body and blood of Christ, that is, with Christ in his state of sacrificial victim. See *(1 Cor 10:15-16).*

Christ is our sacrificial food. To receive his body and blood is to enter into his disposition of total self-offering to the Father; it is to be drawn into the same movement of loving sacrifice. That is what participation means at its deepest level, and it is beautifully expressed by Pope St Leo in the following passage:

> For naught else is effected by the partaking of the Body and Blood of Christ than that we pass into that which we take *(ut in id quod sumimus transeamus),* and both in spirit and in body carry everywhere him in and with whom we were dead, buried and rose again.

Our Good Friday communion therefore proclaims and witnesses to the passion and death of the Lord; it enables us to participate at the deepest level in Christ's sacrifice and to associate ourselves with it; and finally it gives us a share of the fruits of that sacrifice.

When all have received communion, a period of silent prayer is observed; priest and people meditate on the sacrament they have received. We thank the Lord who, in this sacrament, has left us a wonderful memorial of his suffering and death, and also a pledge of future glory.

The service is concluded with the prayer after communion, followed by a prayer of blessing. The former refers to the healing and transforming power of the sacrament; it asks for a generous spirit of service in those who have taken part in the celebration. Among the blessings invoked on the assembly, that of stronger faith is especially important. Faith is the foundation of all the virtues.

The Good Friday liturgy is at an end. There is no dismissal or recessional hymn. People depart in silence. Some remain to continue their own prayers and devotions. Those who did not have an opportunity to kiss the cross may now do so. Others may make the stations of the cross.

The altar is stripped bare, the tabernacle is empty, the sanctuary devoid of flowers or other ornamentation. On no other day of the year are our churches so austere in appearance. Nothing distracts our attention from the altar and the crucifix. The Church keeps vigil by the cross of the Lord.

NOTES

1. *Egeria's Travels,* (ed. John Wilkinson), SPCK, 1971, p. 138.
2. See *New Liturgy* 4, Winter 1974-75, p. 20.
3. See H. Cazelles, "La destinee du Serviteur" in *Le Triduum Pascal,* vol. 21, series *Assemblées du Seigneur,* Cerf, Paris, 1969, pp. 7-15. Also W. Harrington in *Scripture in Church* 14, pp. 211-12.
4. See C. Bourgin, "La Passion du Christ et la nôtre" in *Le Triduum Pascal,* vol. 21 of *Assemblées du Seigneur,* pp. 16-21. Also W. Harrington in *Scripture in Church,* 14, pp. 219-20.
5. Here I follow commentary of I. de la Potterie, "La Passion selon St Jean" in *Le Triduum Pascal,* vol. 21 of *Assemblées du Seigneur,* pp. 22-38.
6. In the fifth century they were part of the daily formula of the Mass. For history see *The Church at Prayer: The Eucharist,* (ed. A. G. Martimort), Irish University Press, 1973, pp. 109-112.
7. *Egeria's Travels,* (ed. John Wilkinson), SPCK, 1971, p. 137. The kissing of the cross is witnessed to in Rome from the seventh century.
8. Composed by Venantius Fortunatus (AD 530-600) on the occasion of the sending of a relic of the true cross to Queen Radegunde for the convent at Poitiers. See J. Connelly, *Hymns of the Roman Liturgy* Longmans, Green and Co., London, 1954, pp. 81-84.
9. Translation of his letters and sermons in vol. XII of the series *Nicene and Post-Nicene Fathers,* Parker and Co., Oxford and New York, 1895.
10. Sermon 72, *Nicene and Post-Nicene Fathers,* vol. 12, p. 184. Pope St Leo here says: "The text of the divinely inspired story has clearly shown the treachery of the Lord Jesus Christ's betrayal, the judgment by which he was condemned, the barbarity of his crucifixion, and the glory of his resurrection."

13

HOLY SATURDAY

On Holy Saturday the Church waits at the Lord's tomb, meditating on his suffering and death. The altar is left bare and the sacrifice of the Mass is not celebrated. Only after the solemn vigil during the night, held in anticipation of the Resurrection, does the Easter celebration begin, with a spirit of joy that overflows into the following period of fifty days.

This introductory note from the missal explains the character of the day. We are to refrain from premature rejoicing as the Easter celebration has not yet begun. It is a day of quiet waiting, or prayerful preparation for the Resurrection. There is still sorrow, even if it lacks the intensity of the preceding day. The early Christians fasted as strictly on this day as on the Friday, for this was the time when Christ the Bridegroom was taken from them *(Mt 2:19-21).*

If we can spend this day in quiet and prayerful waiting, our time will have been well spent. In the beautiful homily, chosen for today's office of readings, it is this mood which is evoked:

> Today there is a great silence on earth; a great silence and then solitude; a great silence because the King sleeps; the earth trembled and was silent, because God has gone to sleep in the flesh, and has awakened those who have slept from of old.

On the first Holy Saturday all seemed lost. The disciples were scattered, a small dispirited band of men, their hopes shattered. Only Mary kept faith and awaited the resurrection of her Son. That is why on Saturdays throughout the year the

93

Church commemorates the Virgin Mary, and there is a votive Mass and office in her honour.

A note of serenity, even of joyful expectancy, pervades the Holy Saturday liturgy. Christ has died, but his death is like a sleep from which he will awake on Easter morning.

The psalms chosen for the office of readings are redolent of quiet trust and expectancy. It is as though Christ himself were praying them. In Psalm 4 the verse "I will lie down in peace and sleep comes at once" is applied to Christ in the tomb confidently awaiting the Resurrection. Again in Psalm 15 we have wonderful expressions of hope: "For you will not leave my soul among the dead, nor let your beloved know decay. You will show me the path of life, the fullness of joy in your presence, at your right hand happiness for ever."

The scripture reading *(Heb 4:1-13)* speaks to us of the Sabbath day of rest prepared for God's people after the labours of this life. It concludes: "There must still be, therefore, a place of rest reserved for God's people, the seventh-day rest, since to reach the place of rest is to rest after your work, as God did after his."

In the ancient homily from which we have already quoted, a dialogue takes place between Christ and Adam. Christ enters the abode of the dead and awakens Adam, saying to him: "Arise from the dead; I am the life of the dead. Arise, O man, work of my hands, arise, you who were fashioned in my image. Rise, let us go hence; for you in me and I in you, together we are one undivided person."

We all share in the mystery of Holy Saturday. St Paul reminds us of this: "When we were baptised we went into the tomb with him and joined him in death, so that as Christ was raised from the dead by the Father's glory, we too might live a new life" *(Rm 6:4)*. In the ancient Church the symbolism of baptism as burial with Christ was more obvious than in later times. Baptism was by immersion; the adult catechumens really went down into the baptismal font which in appearance was not unlike a tomb. They descended into the waters as a sign of death and burial; they emerged from the font signifying the resurrection.

Our participation in the burial of Christ is evoked in the prayers which conclude the office. In the final petition of morning prayer we ask: "Christ, Son of the living God, you enabled us to be buried with you in baptism; grant that, being conformed to your resurrection, we may walk in newness of life." And in the concluding prayer we ask: "Grant that your faithful people, who were buried with him in baptism, may, by his resurrection, obtain eternal life."

14

THE CELEBRATION OF EASTER

With the approach of nightfall we have arrived at the heart of our Holy Week celebrations. It is the hour of the great Vigil, the Easter Vigil, which St Augustine described as "the mother of all vigils".

For the Christians of antiquity Easter was not just one feast among many, it was rather "the feast of feasts". And it was essentially in the night vigil, culminating in the Mass of the Resurrection, that they celebrated this feast.

The Church of our time has rediscovered the deep significance of Easter as the celebration of the paschal mystery. Thanks to the restored rites of Holy Week, begun under Pope Pius XII and completed since Vatican II, the pre-eminence of Easter in the liturgical year is secured. Holy Week constitutes the heart of the liturgical year and the Easter Vigil lies at the heart of Holy Week.

Why is the Easter Vigil so important? Why does the Church urge us to take part in the long-drawn-out liturgy, held at such an inconvenient hour? It is not just because it is ancient and traditional but because of its profound meaning and inner value. Here at the heart of Easter we are celebrating the mystery of human redemption. According to the definition of Odo Casel, Easter, the Christian pasch, is "the feast of human redemption through the death and resurrection of the Lord".[1]

In the course of the liturgical year the Church commemorates the various aspects of the work of redemption. On this occasion it celebrates it as a whole in all its amplitude. This is the paschal feast which includes all the other Christian mysteries. Because of our union with Christ through faith and baptism, we ourselves are intimately associated with the dying and rising of Christ. In celebrating the paschal mystery of Christ, the Church celebrates her own passing-over from death to life.

The Jewish pasch. This most Christian of feasts has its roots in the Old Testament, and to understand it we must first consider the Jewish passover. Divine providence has linked the two celebrations, and even the name "pasch" is of Hebrew origin. (The Latin *pascha,* the French *pâque* and even the Irish *cásc* derive from the Hebrew word.)

The Jewish passover was celebrated on the fourteenth day of the spring month of Nisan. It commemorated the deliverance of the Israelites from their life of oppression and servitude in Egypt. It was a feast of redemption, of liberation. The blood of the lamb, sprinkled on the door posts, underlined its redemptive character; for the destroying angel passed over the households preserved by the blood of the lamb.

In fact this feast contained the memory of all God's wonderful deeds in the course of history; deliverance from the hand of the enemy, the giving of the convenant on Mount Sinai, the wonders of the exodus and final entry into the promised land. It also commemorated the "birth" of God's people. From being an oppressed minority in the land of Egypt, it became a people, a nation, God's "very own possession".

The passover was the great event in the history of Israel. Its commemoration in the yearly paschal festival was the great feast of the Jewish people. We read in chapter twelve of the book of Exodus:

> It is the night of the pasch, the Lord's passing by. . .
> You are to observe this day as a memorial of the past, a
> day when you keep holiday in the Lord's honour. . . It
> is a night for keeping vigil in the Lord's honour, this night
> when he led them out of the land of Egypt.

Its celebration was not merely a recalling of what had happened in the distant past, but a memorial through which the past event became a present reality, and those who celebrated it felt themselves caught up and made sharers in the experience of their forefathers. To the present day, devout Jews celebrate the passover with a keen sense of personal participation, as is evident from the words of their ritual: "It was not our ancestors only, that the most High (blessed be he) redeemed from Egypt, but us also did he redeem with them."

The Christian pasch. It was not by chance that Christ endured his passion and underwent death on our behalf at the time of the Jewish pasch. It is part of a divine plan and of a divine pedagogy. In his sacrifice on the cross Christ is shown to be the fulfilment of the ancient passover. In the words of St Paul, "Christ, our passover, has been sacrificed" *(1 Cor 5:7).*

Among the New Testament writers St John takes special care to show the correspondence between the events of the passover and the mysteries of Christ's life. He shows, for example, how Christ fulfils the major types of the exodus. He is the new Moses leading his people to freedom; he feeds them with the new manna which is the Eucharist; he gives them to drink from the fountain of living water. He is the bronze serpent and all who look upon him with faith are saved. He is the light shining in the darkness, a more perfect light than that which led the Israelites through the desert. He is the true paschal lamb.[2]

St John begins his account of the Last Supper with the words which evoke the passover and its celebration: "It was before the festival of the passover, and Jesus knew that the hour had come for him to pass from this world to the Father" *(Jn 13:1).* In this mysterious passage Christ achieves a more wonderful deliverance than that of Moses. In his passing through death from this world to the Father, Christ delivers all men from the servitude of sin.

The passion narrative of St John is full of Old Testament reminiscences, quite a few of which relate to the passover celebration. According to John, it is at the hour of the evening sacrifice, when the paschal lambs are being slain in the Temple, that Jesus is crucified. John also tells us that in fulfilment of what was said of the paschal lamb the soldiers did not break his legs:

99

"Not a bone of his shall be broken." (See *Exodus 12:46.*)

Easter then is the true paschal feast, it celebrates the paschal mystery of Christ and his Church. It is a feast of redemption, and it is especially in the liturgy of the Easter Vigil that the Church celebrates that feast. In it we celebrate Christ's victory over sin and death, his opening up to mankind of a new life in God. Through our sharing in his death and resurrection, we ourselves gain access to the kingdom of light and freedom.

The vigil service. The vigil is divided into four parts: a service of light; a Liturgy of the Word; a baptismal service; the paschal Eucharist.

Service of Light. The theme of light is a constant one in the Easter liturgy. It is appropriate that the Vigil should begin with the blessing of the Easter fire and the lighting of the paschal candle.

Ideally, the service will begin outside the church, in front of the porch, where a large fire has been prepared. The people gather round the fire in a circle. Easter is a complete new beginning for the world. That is the symbolism of the new fire and the new light.

This fire ritual is pre-Christian, but because of its rich symbolism it has been assumed into the Church's liturgy. Here in Ireland, we may associate the Easter fire with that which St Patrick is said to have lit one Easter evening on the Hill of Slane before appearing in the presence of King Laoghaire at Tara.[3] However, if there are pagan vestiges in this ritual, they are at once dispelled by the opening words of the priest:

> Dear friends in Christ,
> on this most holy night,
> when our Lord Jesus Christ passed from death
> to life,
> the Church invites her children
> throughout the world
> to come together in vigil and prayer
> This is the passover of the Lord. . .

The new fire is blessed; from it the paschal candle will be lit. Attention now turns to this candle, an extra large and beautiful one, which throughout the whole Easter season, will serve as a symbol of Christ.

To fit it out for its symbolic role, the candle may be suitably marked, following medieval tradition. First the priest cuts a cross in the wax with a stylus. Then he traces the Greek letter *Alpha* above the cross and the letter *Omega* below. These are the first and last letters of the Greek alphabet. "I am the alpha and omega, the first and the last, the beginning and the end", says Christ in the Book of Revelation *(22:13)*.

Between the arms of the cross the numerals of the current year, e.g. 1984, are inscribed. Christ is thus shown to be the "King of all ages". For us Christians, every year is a year of the Lord, since we profess that all times and seasons belong to him. In the formula accompanying the incisions, the priest says:

> Christ yesterday and today
> the beginning and the end
> Alpha and Omega
> all times belong to him
> and all ages
> to him be glory and power
> through every age and for ever. Amen.

The priest may now insert five grains of incense in the candle to represent the wounds the Saviour received on head, feet, hands and side. This he does in the form of a cross, saying: "By his holy and glorious wounds may Christ our Lord guard us and keep us."

The candle is lit from the new fire with the words: "May the light of Christ, rising in glory, dispel the darkness of our hearts and minds."

Then a procession forms. The priest or deacon takes the Easter candle, lifts it high and acclaims: "Christ our light", to which all respond: "Thanks be to God." Then all enter the darkened church, led by the candle-bearer.

At the church door the candle is lifted high a second time, again with the acclamation "Christ, our light" and the response "Thanks be to God." At this point all the members of the congregation have their small candles lit from the flame of the paschal candle. This conveys the idea that the light, which is Christ, must be communicated. This happens when the Gospel is preached, when men accept it with faith and are baptised. Faith is a gift of God, but, as the human instruments of God, we help to mediate that faith to others.

When the priest or deacon carrying the candle arrives before the altar, he turns round to face the people and makes his acclamation for the third and last time. The people take their places in the pews and the lights of the church are put on. The candle is placed on its stand in the sanctuary.

The Easter Song of Praise, also known as the *Exultet,* now follows. As the Latin word suggests, it is a hymn of joy and exultation in praise of God, the author of light and the giver of life and salvation. It was the custom among the Jews to say a prayer of blessing at the time of lighting the evening lamp in the home. This custom was taken over into Christian usage, and the Church's evening prayer, known in early times as *lucernarium* (from *lucerna,* a lamp), developed out of it. The magnificent formula of praise and blessing said before the paschal candle is but an elaborate form of what was commonplace in Christian antiquity.

It begins with a three-fold invitation to rejoice: "Rejoice, heavenly powers, Rejoice, O earth, Rejoice, O Mother Church". It is, of course, the redemption of mankind, in all its phases and aspects that is the cause of the Church's rejoicing.

The whole of salvation history is there in poetic form: the passover of the Hebrews, of Christ and of the Church. The great wax candle evokes at once the pillar of fire that led the Israelites across the desert and Christ the Light of the world; it is the light of revelation, of baptism and of final glory.

The *Exultet* is one of the literary and theological treasures of the Roman liturgy. In it, praise, thanksgiving and supplication are blended in a splendid unity. Ideally it should be sung; the vernacular text has been set to music.[4] It is accorded the same honours as the proclamation of the gospel. All remain standing holding their lighted candles while it is being sung.

The Liturgy of the Word. After the Easter Song of Praise the candles are put out and all sit down for the Liturgy of the Word. This consists of readings, canticles and prayers. The reading of the word of God is ''the fundamental element of the Easter vigil''. There are nine readings altogether, culminating in the gospel of the Mass. For pastoral reasons the number of readings may be reduced, but it should be borne in mind that the Church attaches great importance to these readings.[5]

To relieve monotony it is preferable to have several readers. Good readers can make a scriptural text come alive. The Old Testament readings, in particular, lend themselves to a certain dramatic interpretation.

The whole atmosphere in which this service of readings is carried out should be relaxed and unhurried. We must dispose ourselves to listen attentively to the word of God. Here is set before us a whole synopsis of salvation history, God's great plan to redeem the world. In the books of the Old Testament that plan unfolds itself; in the New Testament it finds realisation. It is the story of God's love for the world.

First reading. The first reading is the account of creation *(Gen 1:1 – 2:2).* There is great optimism in the Old Testament vision of creation and in the repeated refrain, ''God saw that it was good''. Creation mirrored the perfections of God himself.

But the God of creation is also the God of redemption. In admiring his handiwork in nature, the Church is drawn to contemplate his wonders in the order of grace. For this is a baptismal vigil: on this night the sacrament of re-birth is conferred or renewed. And even in this first reading Christian tradition finds a baptismal typology. The Spirit of God that ''hovered over the water'' in the beginning is the same Holy Spirit who sanctifies the waters of baptism. The creation of light on the first day also suggests baptism, the sacrament of enlightenment.

Baptism is a new creation. We read in *Genesis* how God

103

created man in his own image. This image was disfigured by sin and needed to be restored by Christ's redeeming work. Through faith and baptism that redemption becomes operative in us. St Paul reminds the newly-baptised: "You have stripped off your old behaviour with your old self, and you have put on a new self which will progress towards true knowledge the more it is renewed in the image of its maker" *(Col 3:10)*. Elsewhere he says: "Therefore, if anyone is in Christ, he is a new creation; the old has passed away, behold, the new has come" *(2 Cor 5:17)*.

In this liturgical reading of the Old Testament we are operating, so to speak, on two levels. The Church reads into this account of creation the mystery of recreation, that is, of redemption. This is made explicit in the prayer which follows the reading and psalm:

> Almighty and eternal God,
> you created all things
>   in wonderful beauty and order.
> Help us now to perceive
> how still more wonderful is the new creation
> by which in the fullness of time
> you redeemed your people
> through the sacrifice of our passover,
>   Jesus Christ.

Second reading. The restoration of this reading *(Gen 22:1-18)* to the Easter Vigil liturgy (from which it had been dropped in a previous reform) has been greatly appreciated. Christian tradition has always attached it closely to the paschal mystery, and in the Old Testament it was read in the context of the passover.[6]

Briefly, it recounts how Abraham, in obedience to a divine command, prepares to sacrifice his only and much-loved son, Isaac. At the last moment an angel appears and orders him not to raise his hand against the boy. It was his obedience that was being put to the test. Instead of his son, a ram is offered as a burnt sacrifice. In conclusion, Abraham is promised the reward of his obedience: he will become the father of many nations.

Abraham would not even spare his beloved child Isaac. We find echoes of this in the New Testament with reference to Christ. St John tell us: "Yes, God loved the world so much that he gave his only Son, so that everyone who believes in him may not be lost but have eternal life" *(Jn 3:16).* This was a more perfect sacrifice since God spared Isaac but did not spare his own son. However, God's mercy did not detract from Abraham's unconditional obedience which prefigured that of Christ himself, who was "obedient unto death". Isaac, too, is a "type" of Christ. Not only is he innocent, but willingly allows himself to be sacrificed. Christ offers no resistance to his captors; he is led like a sheep to slaughter.

If the sacrifice of Christ is foreshadowed here, so is his resurrection. The author of *Hebrews* alludes to this: "By faith Abraham, when he was tested, offered up Isaac. . . He considered that God was able to raise men even from the dead; hence he did receive him back, and this was a symbol" *(Heb 11:17-20; RSV version).*

Finally, we may consider how fruitful was the obedience of Abraham: God would shower blessings upon him; his descendants would be as numerous as the stars of heaven and as the grains of sand on the seashore. How much more fruitful is the sacrifice of Christ by which the world is reconciled with God, and men and women are united as children of the one Father. It is through the sacrifice of Christ that the promises made to Abraham are fulfilled. (See concluding prayer.)

Third reading. So important is this reading *(Ex 14:15 – 15:1)* for an understanding of the paschal mystery that it may not be omitted. It describes the miraculous crossing of the Red Sea by the Israelites. This was the great breakthrough to freedom of God's people, an event of decisive importance in their history.

Here redemption is presented as a victory. The crossing of the Red Sea was a disaster for Pharaoh and his army; for the Israelites it was a triumph and deliverance. It symbolised the victory of God over the powers of evil.

The redemption accomplished by Christ was also a victory; and it was as a victory that the early fathers of the Church liked to understand it. It was a battle fought between Christ and his adversary, Satan. Here goodness was pitted against evil, light against darkness: ''Death with life contended: combat strangely ended! Life's own champion, slain, yet lives to reign'' (Sequence for Easter Sunday). From this struggle, in which at first Satan seems to triumph, Christ emerges victorious.

Through baptism the Christian shares in the victory of Christ. The waters of baptism are a force for life and death: life for those who are cleansed by these waters, death to all that is opposed to the reign of God. Like the Israelites of old, the newly-baptised pass through the waters of the Red Sea: they leave behind them the world of darkness and slavery and with Christ (the new Moses) at their head, they set out for the promised land.

It will be noted that the responsorial psalm is actually a continuation of the reading. Here the narrative breaks into song: ''I will sing to the Lord, glorious his triumph!'' It is the victory song of the people of God, the canticle of Moses and the sons of Israel. It is also the victory song of the people of God of the New Testament; it is the thanksgiving song of those whom Christ has redeemed. On Easter night we sing it with exultation. St John heard it sung in the New Jerusalem: ''They all had harps from God, and they were singing the hymn of Moses the servant of God, and of the Lamb'' *(Rev 15:3).*

The covenant theme. The next four readings, all from the Prophets, may be grouped together under the theme of covenant. They speak of God's redeeming love, of the everlasting covenant he has made with his people; they exhort us to be faithful to that covenant, to give our wholehearted allegiance to the Law of God.

The fourth reading *(Is 54:5-14)* expresses the covenant relationship between God and his people. It is no mere legal arrangement, but resembles rather the marriage contract. It is a partnership of love which demands mutual trust, generosity and fidelity. Where these qualities are lacking, the relationship is under strain. It can break down completely if either party is unfaithful.

Time and again Israel has been unfaithful to the marriage contract between God and his people, but God never annulled that contract nor disowned the unfaithful spouse. His love conquers. Where there has been alienation there is now reconciliation. How beautifully this is expressed in the lines:

> In excess of anger, for a moment
> I hid my face from you.
> But with everlasting love
>   I have taken pity on you,
> says the Lord, your redeemer.

God reaffirms the marriage contract. He swears that his love will never depart from his people; his "covenant of peace" will never be shaken.

This reading draws attention to a fundamental aspect of the redemption, namely, the divine love which inspired it. Love, undeserved and unreciprocated, is the ultimate explanation and the motive-force of man's redemption. In celebrating the feast of human redemption at Easter we are brought face to face with the mystery of divine love.

Again in the fifth reading *(Is 55:1-11)* we meet the covenant idea, but now the accent is more on our response to the covenant than on the "divine pity".

"With you I will make an everlasting covenant", says the Lord. In the Old Testament the passover feast commemorated, among other marvels, the giving of the covenant. For the Church of the New Testament, Easter celebrates the establishment of the "new and eternal covenant" which was sealed in the blood of Christ. In Christ, the mediator of that covenant, all the promises made to the patriarchs and prophets are fulfilled.

As God's people, we must be faithful to the terms of the covenant. The giving must not be all on God's side. His love and fidelity must be answered by our love and fidelity; otherwise there is no real covenant relationship. Christ is our model: as head of redeemed humanity he offered to the Father the perfect response of obedience and love.

In the sixth reading *(Bar 3:9-15, 32 – 4:4)* the prophet, as spokesman of God, makes an impassioned appeal to Israel to be converted and to return to the Lord. His words challenge us as they challenged the Jewish nation in the time of the Babylonian captivity.

Conversion must be expressed in a ready acceptance of the Law of God. This means that our lives must correspond with that law and be in conformity with it. That is another way of saying that we must keep our part of the covenant.

For us Christians this means living according to the Gospel of Christ in which the Old Law finds its fulfilment. It demands of us not only the acceptance of individual commandments but our willingness to live according to the spirit of the New Law.

The prophet Baruch presents us with a beautiful and compelling vision of a life lived in accordance with the Law. It is a life blessed with peace, strength and happiness. The Law is not something legalistic and narrowly conceived, but a whole way of life. It is the embodiment and living expression of wisdom.

The seventh and final Old Testament reading *(Ezk 36:16-28)* contains God's promise to pardon his unfaithful people, to gather them from among the nations and restore them to their own land. Redemption is here seen as a work of restoration and reunification. Sin is the cause of division and dispersal. Christ, redeemer of mankind, has effected a more perfect restoration: he has gathered people of all nations into the unity of his body; between Christ and his members no closer unity could be conceived.

Then there is a prophetic utterance which again sounds the theme of baptism: "I shall pour clean water over you and you will be cleansed." The Church fathers saw in this an allusion to the purifying waters of baptism. The responsorial psalm, with its refrain "Like the deer that longs for running streams. . .", expresses the longing of the catechumen for the sacrament of baptism.

The concluding part of the reading is taken up with the covenant theme. Henceforth God's law will be obeyed not just in a literal way but from the heart. This is made possible by the fact that God will transform the human heart, making it capable of generous response. A relationship which is even more intimate than that of natural kinship is thus established between God and man. This is the true covenant relationship, expressed in those words which appear as a kind of refrain in the Bible: "You shall be my people and I will be your God."

The prayer which follows the seventh reading may be considered as a summing up of the whole series of Old Testament readings. There is a choice of two prayers. The first expresses the plea that God may carry forward and bring to completion the work of redemption begun long ago; it is a prayer for renewal for the Church and mankind. The second formula asks for a deeper understanding of the love which motivated the passover mystery.

Easter glory. It sometimes happens that at the end of a long journey we are rather taken by surprise that we have reached our destination. One may have a similar experience on Holy Saturday night. The transition from Old Testament prophecy to the full splendour of Easter is sudden and almost imperceptible. After the seventh reading, with its responsory and prayer, the altar candles are lighted for Mass. There is no break in the sequence, but a gentle transition from darkness to light. The waiting is over, Easter has now arrived.

The celebrant intones the *Gloria,* that joyful prose-hymn which we have inherited from Christian antiquity. It is recited or chanted at every festive Mass outside Lent. Traditionally it is closely associated with Easter, for, according to ancient Roman custom, it could be said or sung by ordinary priests only at the Mass of the Vigil.[7] It expresses praise, adoration and humble supplication. To heighten the note of joy, the bells of the Church may be rung, heralding far and wide the good news of the Resurrection.

This is followed by the opening prayer of the Mass. The grace we ask for is that of the spirit of sonship and of renewal; thus renewed, we shall be enabled to offer God the wholehearted service which is his due.

The first of the New Testament readings is taken from the letter of St Paul to the Romans *(6:3-11)*. The apostle penetrates to the heart of the Easter mystery. He explains how, through the sacrament of baptism, we participate in the paschal mystery of Christ. Christ, our head, suffered, died, was buried and rose again. Through baptismal grace, we, the body, are made to share, in a real and most intimate way, in this mysterious passage from death to life.

Baptism is a new beginning. The old way of life is left behind. It confers on us the status of children of God. Henceforth we share in the life of the risen Christ. Christian moral conduct must now accord with the dignity of our calling. Our life must be lived in and with Christ for God our Father. This calls for a new attitude, a new orientation and sense of purpose. In this short reading a whole programme of Christian living opens out for us.

The Easter Alleluia. After the reading all rise and the priest solemnly intones the *Alleluia* which is repeated by the congregation. This acclamation, so expressive of praise, joy and victory makes its return after the long period of Lent during which it was muted. No other acclamation is so characteristic of the Easter season than this single Hebrew word. Ideally it will be sung, and there is a beautiful plain chant melody to accompany it.

In his Easter homilies St Augustine never tired of expounding the significance of the *Alleluia,* the cry which anticipates the liturgy of heaven. Here it heralds the gospel of the Resurrection and Christ himself who is present and speaks to us in his word. That is the function of the *Alleluia* at every Mass, but it acquires its full significance on this night of Easter.

The *Alleluia,* thrice repeated, forms the people's refrain after each strophe of the responsorial psalm. The psalm chosen is the great Easter psalm, *Psalm 117.* Christian tradition has closely allied it to the Easter mystery, and for that reason we meet it constantly throughout the paschal season. As used in the liturgy of this time, it sings of the victory of the risen Christ, which is also the victory of those whom he has redeemed. Catechumens about to be received into the Church, sinners restored to grace, the whole people of God renewed by the discipline of Lent, all can make their own those words of the psalm which tradition applies to Christ in his resurrection: ''The Lord's right hand has triumphed, his right hand raised me up. I shall not die, I shall live and recount his deeds.''

The gospel of the resurrection. The word gospel comes from an Old English word "godspel" which means good tidings. The gospel is indeed the good news of salvation, and the gospel of the Resurrection which we hear on Easter night is the most joyful in the whole year.

The present lectionary provides that, in the course of the three-year cycle, we will hear in turn the resurrection narrative of Matthew, Mark and Luke. The gospel account according to John is read at the day-time Mass.

With good reason the Church has found a place for each gospel. Each sacred author describes what happened in his own way. The central message, however, is the same in each.

In Matthew's account, an angel tells the women: "I know you are looking for Jesus, who was crucified. He is not here, for he has risen, as he said he would." In the gospel of Mark a young man in a white robe declares to the three women: "You are looking for Jesus of Nazareth, who was crucified: he has risen, he is not here." Luke has two men in brilliant clothes who ask: "Why look among the dead for someone who is alive? He is not here, he is risen."

It is the fact of the Resurrection, rather than the events surrounding it, which commands our faith. We believe and profess that Christ rose from the dead on Easter Sunday. That lies at the very heart of our Christian faith.

In the Easter liturgy the evangelists speak to us, and Christ speaks to us through them. The Church allows the gospels to speak for themselves without adornment or qualification. And the best disposition to hear and to benefit from the liturgical readings is to lay ourselves open to them with a simple faith and a readiness to obey their message.

The gospel of the resurrection (whether it is Matthew, Mark, Luke or John who is addressing us) is a message for here and now. It may be familiar to us all, but can we pretend to have fathomed the mystery to which it points? It challenges our faith, it invites serious thought about the very foundations of our Christian religion.

The Resurrection is not only an event of history, it is an ever-present reality which affects the life of each one of us. It has changed the course of history and it can transform our lives.

The baptismal liturgy. The celebration of the paschal mystery at Easter provides the most appropriate setting for the conferring of baptism. From as early as the second century the baptism of adult catechumens was linked with Easter; and even after the disappearance of the adult catechumenate in the sixth century, it continued to be the practice of the Roman Church for many centuries to baptise infants at Easter or at Pentecost.[8] In our own time this ancient practice has been revived; and it is not such a rare thing to have an adult or child baptised in the course of the Easter Vigil.

If there are candidates for baptism, the priest now invites the assembly to pray for them. At the moment of their reception into full membership of the Christian community, earnest intercession is made on their behalf; and as on similar occasions (ordinations, religious professions) when the candidates are about to embark on a new state of life, the Litany of the Saints is said or sung to invoke God's abundant blessing on them.

In this litany the Church on earth associates her prayer with that of the Church in heaven. Christ, his angels and saints are invoked on behalf of these "chosen ones" who now approach the waters of re-birth. The litany is representative of the great saints of every age, including our own. There is a special petition for those about to be baptised: "Give new life to these chosen ones by the grace of baptism."

The water itself must now be prepared by a solemn prayer of blessing. In this beautiful formula, which dates from the sixth century or earlier, there is set before us a biblical reflection on the mystery of baptism. The themes we met in the readings, e.g. the water that covered the earth in the beginning, the crossing of the Red Sea, recur here. They are completed by New Testament additions such as the baptism of Christ in the Jordan, the blood and water that flowed from his side on the cross.

The Holy Spirit, who hovered over the waters at the dawn of creation, who in the form of a dove descended on Jesus in the Jordan, is now invoked to sanctify the baptismal font. Water is the material agent by which, through the power of the Holy

112

Spirit, man is purified from sin and vice and engendered to a new life. The baptismal font is the tomb in which we are buried to sin; it is also the maternal womb from which we are reborn as children of God.

The role of the Holy Spirit in sanctifying the water is forcefully evoked by the rite of plunging the paschal candle three times into the font, with the invocation: "We ask you, Father, with your son to send the Holy Spirit upon the waters of this font." It is held in the water until the completion of the blessing.

The moment for baptism has now arrived. It is to be hoped that there will be some candidate or candidates, whether infant or adult. To be baptised on this particular night is to participate in a very special way in the celebration of the paschal mystery; the passage from death to life, symbolised and effected by baptism, coincides with the liturgical celebration of that mystery.

We are all now given the opportunity to renew and consolidate our baptismal commitment. This is one of the summits of the Easter celebration, one prepared for throughout the whole period of Lent.

All present stand with lighted candles and, at the invitation of the priest, renew their baptismal profession of faith. They first renounce Satan, his works and empty promises. They then profess their faith in the articles of the Creed.

This rite of renewal somehow knits the community together. All of us, whether priests, religious or lay persons, are united in the profession of one faith; we form one people of God; we are all God's faithful, that is, a people established in the profession of their baptismal faith.

It was all so easy at our own baptism. The sponsors made that profession for us. But to make that faith our own and to live by it in adult life is not easy. Our faith may have to withstand difficulties of all kinds, but we are given the grace to say and to mean "I do believe". The grace of Easter is the grace of a faith newly found. We not only profess that faith but also pledge ourselves to live by it, which means rejecting all that is contrary to our life in Christ.

Having concluded with a prayer, the priest sprinkles the

people with the blessed water, thus reminding them again of their own baptism. During the rite of sprinkling some suitable baptismal chant may be sung.

The eucharistic liturgy. The eucharistic liturgy begins in the usual way with the presentation of the gifts. A rubric recommends that the bread and wine be brought to the altar by the newly-baptised, who are specially honoured since this is the Mass of their first communion.

The Eucharist completes the divine work begun in us at baptism. Together with the sacrament of confirmation it completes the process of Christian initiation. It only remains for us to co-operate with divine grace in bringing this process to full maturity. We must by our moral conduct, aligned to the Gospel and sustained by the sacraments, "become what we are", that is, grow into the full realisation of our status as adopted sons and daughters of God. This idea of completion is evoked in the prayer over the gifts: "May this Easter mystery of our redemption bring to perfection the saving mystery you have begun in us."

The particular significance of our Easter Mass and communion is the theme of the first preface:

> We praise you with greater joy than ever
> on this Easter night
> when Christ became our paschal sacrifice.
> He is the true Lamb who took away
>   the sins of the world.
> By dying he destroyed our death;
> by rising he restored our life.

This paschal note is again sounded in the Old Roman canon (eucharistic Prayer I) which has appropriate insertions for the feast. The prayer known as the *Communicantes* begins: "In union with the whole Church we celebrate that day (night) when Jesus Christ, our Lord, rose from the dead in his human body."

The newly-baptised are singled out for mention: "Father, accept this offering from your whole family and from those born into the new life of water and the Holy Spirit with all their sins

114

forgiven." This text draws attention to the powers conferred on us through baptism. This sacrament imparts to all its recipients a share in the priesthood of Christ and this enables them to participate in the offering of the eucharistic sacrifice.[9]

Active participation in the Eucharist has its most perfect expression in sacramental communion. Through our sharing in the body and blood of Christ we are brought into the closest union with the sacrifice of our High Priest. This realisation finds joyful expression in the communion antiphon: "Christ has become our paschal sacrifice; let us feast with the unleavened bread of sincerity and truth, alleluia."

In the prayer after communion the grace asked for is that of unity:

> Lord, you have nourished us
>   with your Easter sacraments.
> Fill us with the Spirit of your love
> and make us all one in heart.

This is the intention for which Christ prayed at the Last Supper: "that they may be one" *(Jn 17:11)*. This was the object of his sacrificial death, "to gather into one the children of God who are scattered abroad", and to draw all things to himself *(Jn 11:52; 12:32)*. This unity is perfected by the Holy Spirit who unites all the followers of Christ and forms them into his Body the Church. It is in receiving the body and blood of Christ that we are filled with his Holy Spirit and become one body and one spirit with him. (See eucharistic Prayer III.)

Our Easter communion has made us more effective instruments of God's peace and love. Our mission is to spread the good news of his divine love and to work for the fulfilment of God's loving purpose in the world. It is to this task that we are sent forth by the words of the priest: "Go in peace to love and serve the Lord, alleluia, alleluia."

Commemoration of our Lady. According to an ancient belief, Jesus, after his resurrection, first appeared to his mother Mary. This appearance is not recorded in the gospels; yet it would indeed have been very fitting.[10] Whether we accept it or not, it has given rise to a beautiful custom preserved in some monastic communities.

At the conclusion of the Mass of the Easter Vigil, the celebrant, ministers and community file out in solemn procession from the sanctuary. At a specially prepared place in the church a picture or sculpture of Our Lady of Sorrows has been set in position surrounded by flowers. Here the procession halts. The monks turn to face the *pietà*. A chanter intones the *Regina Coeli* and this is taken up by the whole community. As Christ is supposed to have conveyed the joyful tidings of his resurrection first to his mother on Easter morning, so the Church now relives that scene in the words of the anthem:

> Joy fill your heart, O Queen most high, alleluia!
> Your Son who in the tomb did lie, alleluia!
> Has risen as he did prophesy, alleluia!

NOTES

1.   Dom Odo Casel, *La Fête de Pâques dans l'Eglise des Pères,* vol. 37, series *Lex Orandi,* Cerf, Paris, 1963, p. 93. This is a translation from the German.
2.   See *John 6:31-32; 7:37-39; 3:13-15; 8:12-13; 19:33-37.*
3.   See J. Walton Tyrer, *Historical Survey of Holy Week,* Alcuin Club Collections, No. XXIX, Oxford University Press, 1932, pp. 148-49.
4.   *The Exultet,* English text set to music by a monk of Glenstal, Liturgical Publications, Glenstal Abbey, Ireland.
5.   "At least three readings from the Old Testament should be read, although for more serious reasons the number may be reduced to two. The reading of *Exodus 14,* however, is never to be omitted."
6.   See J. Bernard, "L'institution eucharistique" in *Jeudi Saint,* vol. 20 of *Assemblées du Seigneur,* pp. 48-49.
7.   See *The Church at Prayer: The Eucharist,* (ed. A. G. Martimort), Irish University Press, 1973, p. 88.
8.   See J. A. Jungmann, "The History of Holy Week" in *Studies in Pastoral Liturgy,* vol. 1, (ed. Placid Murray, OSB), The Furrow Trust, Maynooth, 1961, p. 13. Also *L'Eglise en Prière,* (ed. A. G. Martimort), Desclée, Tournai, 1965, p. 541.
9.   See *General Instruction on the Roman Missal,* chapter 3, no. 62. CTS edition, London, 1973.
10.   Cardinal Newman, among others, held this belief. The poet Rainer Maria Rilke wrote a beautiful poem entitled "The Consolation of Mary with the Risen Christ" which is inspired by this tradition. See *The Penguin Book of Lieder,* (ed. S. Prawer), pp. 176-77.

The traditional greeting of Russian and other Eastern-rite Christians when they meet at Easter, is: "The Lord has risen", to which the reply is "He has truly risen." This is certainly a more expressive exchange of greeting than the banal "Happy Easter!" It is only in the liturgy that we find appropriate expressions of the joy of Easter. The refrain for the invitatory psalm at the morning office corresponds to the Russian greeting: "The Lord has truly risen, alleluia."

In the course of time customs of various kinds have grown round the great religious festivals, in particular Christmas and Easter. One such custom in Irish tradition deserves attention.[1] It was the practice, especially in rural areas, for people to get up early on this Sunday morning to see the sun "dancing". It seems to me that this idea and the customs attached to it can be given a Christian interpretation, namely, that the whole of creation has a share in the joy of the Resurrection. This is borne out by St Paul: "Creation still retains the hope of being freed, like us, from its slavery to decadence to enjoy the same freedom and glory as the children of God" *(Rm 8:19-23)*. The redemption, won by Christ, extends to the whole universe.

The Mass. The Church assembles a second time, now in the full light of day, to celebrate the Easter Eucharist. The Easter candle, prominent on its high stand, is lighted. The sanctuary is adorned with flowers. White vestments symbolise joy, and it is with an expression of rejoicing that the entrance antiphon begins: "I have risen, I am with you once more; you have placed your hand on me to keep me safe. How great is the depth of your wisdom!" How skilfully the Church employs the psalms to express both the sorrows and the joy of Christ. Here it is Christ who speaks, addressing the Father. He is now risen, has now returned to the Father. This is the cry of victory of the *whole* Christ, head and members. In the words of one of the Easter Vigil prayers, the fallen are lifted up, the old are made new and all things brought to perfection.[2]

The opening prayer of the Mass asks for a renewal in our

moral lives corresponding to the mystery of the Resurrection: "Let our celebration today raise us up and renew our lives by the Spirit that is within us." The alternative prayer expresses the same idea in a different form: "May the risen Lord breathe on our minds and open our eyes that we may know him in the breaking of bread, and follow him in his risen life."

In the first reading, from the *Acts of the Apostles (10:34, 37-43)*, it is St Peter who addresses us. He bears witness to the resurrection of Jesus. In fact his discourse gives a résumé of the public life of our Lord, beginning with his baptism by John; every event of that life is shown to have saving power. The culmination of that life is the death and resurrection of the Lord.

The reality of the Resurrection is strongly affirmed. Not only by the statement, "three days afterwards God raised him to life", but also by the assertion that after the Resurrection the apostles had "eaten and drunk" with him. St Peter, the chief apostle, testifies to all this. He speaks as an eye-witness, but he also speaks from the experience of his personal faith enlightened by the Holy Spirit. This apostolic witness is important for our own acceptance of the faith. This discourse of Peter is not only a recounting of what happened in the life of Christ, it is a profession of faith, a proclamation of Christian belief.

This reading also contains the message that the salvation, won by Christ, is universal in scope: "All who believe in Jesus will have their sins forgiven through his name." Through faith all men have access to the saving power of his death and resurrection.

In the second reading St Paul, addressing the Colossian Christians *(Col 3:1-4)*, exhorts them to live in accordance with their newly-acquired state. The resurrection of our bodies and the glory which is to be ours remains an object of hope; but through our intimate union with Christ we already enjoy a foretaste of our inheritance.

While still pilgrims on this earth we must constantly seek the Lord, for he is our life: "Let your thoughts be on heavenly things, not on the things that are on earth." However, St Paul is not urging us to neglect our human tasks or the people with whom we live. That would be a false spirituality. We must be fully involved in the life of this world without being immersed in it or captivated by it. We must realise that our ultimate goal, our final destiny, is not here in this material world, but ''hidden away with Christ in God'', and that we await his coming and manifestation in order that our own true lives may be revealed.

The lectionary provides an alternative reading from the first letter of St Paul to the Corinthians *(5:7-8),* in which he exhorts them to live lives of ''sincerity and truth'' since Christ our passover has been sacrificed.

The sequence, *Victimae paschali,* is a medieval composition which, in dramatic form, sums up the mystery of redemption. Sung to the plain chant melody, it conveys something of the excitement of the first Easter Sunday. It has the form of a hurried dialogue between ourselves and Mary Magdalene. Mary bears witness to what she has seen; and we, believers and disciples, also bear witness: ''That Christ is truly risen from the dead we know.'' (We may note how the theme of victorious combat, so dear to the early Church fathers, recurs in the sequence.)

The gospel is that of St John *(20:1-9).* Again we meet Mary Magdalene, arriving at the tomb ''very early on the first day of the week'' and discovering that it is empty. Her first reaction is one of consternation. She hurries off to tell the two disciples who, on hearing her report, vie with each other in racing to the tomb. John arrives first but allows Peter to enter the tomb first.

''Then the other disciple who had reached the tomb first also went in; he saw and he believed.'' This seeing and believing constitutes the climax of the gospel. The proclamation of the Easter gospel is intended to arouse in each liturgical gathering the same response of faith. This faith rests on the testimony of the apostles and on the inspired scriptures which reveal the plan of God.[3]

Today's celebration should make us more conscious of the paschal character of every Mass. The acclamations, with which we are so familiar, acquire a new depth of meaning at Easter-time. Thus, the acclamation, ''Christ has died, Christ is risen, Christ will come again'', seems most appropriate on this day. It echoes the Easter preface: "By dying he destroyed our death; by rising he restored our life." In the same preface Christ is designated as "the true Lamb who took away the sins of the world", which anticipates what the priest announces before communion: "This is the Lamb of God who takes away the sins of the world."

Our participation in the sacrifice and sacrament of the Mass enables us to live out more truly and more effectively the mystery begun in us at baptism. In the words of J. M. Tillard: "By his change of heart and repentance he (the Christian) enters into the death of Jesus; by the new quality of his acts and life he enters into the Resurrection. Such is the paschal law of the Christian mystery."[4]

Finally, there is the eschatological note, high-lighted in the liturgy of Easter, but never absent from the Church's celebration of the Eucharist: every time we eat this bread and drink this cup we proclaim the death of the Lord until he comes *(1 Cor 11:26)*. At the prayer following the consecration (the *anamnesis*) we commemorate not only past mysteries but look forward to the Lord's coming in glory. Today's liturgy impresses on our minds what we already know, that the Eucharist is the pledge of eternal life, the pledge of our own future resurrection. The sacred banquet of the Eucharist is a foretaste of the eternal paschal feast: "Happy are those who are called to his supper!", that is, "to the wedding feast of the Lamb" *(Rev 19:9)*.

It is on this note of joyful expectation that the prayer after communion sums up our hopes and petitions: "Father of love, watch over your Church, and bring us to the glory of the resurrection promised by this Easter sacrament."

The solemn blessing, which may be used in the Easter season, also directs our thoughts to future glory: "May he fulfil his promises and bless you with eternal life. . . May you come to the feast which lasts forever."

The evening of Easter Sunday has many associations for us. It recalls for us, in the first place, the appearance of the Lord to the two disciples on the road to Emmaus, recorded in the gospel of St Luke *(24:13-35)*. These two men walk along despondently; they do not recognise the stranger who joins them on the road. Together they discuss all that had happened in those last days. Jesus rebukes them for their lack of faith, and then explains to them how everything foretold in the scriptures had come about. Arriving at the inn, they invite their companion to join them for a meal and to remain with them for the night. And then, in the course of the meal, their eyes are opened and they ''recognised him at the breaking of bread''.

If there is an evening Mass on Easter Sunday the gospel reading may be that of St Luke, as described above.[5] It is appropriate that this passage should be read this Sunday evening; even if it does not figure in the liturgy, we should not omit it in our own reading of the scriptures.

''Stay with us, Lord, for evening is approaching and the day is almost over.'' The Church makes this pressing invitation her own. It is an appeal to the Lord to abide with his people, to protect his community. It is a cry which is heard frequently in the liturgy of paschaltide.[6] It arouses in us those sentiments so movingly expressed in the poem of H. F. Lyte, ''Abide with me; fast falls the eventide'' (See appendix to the Divine Office, no. 112).[7]

With second Vespers of Easter Sunday, the paschal triduum is brought to a close. This evening office of praise, thanksgiving and petition provides a prayerful finale to the day's celebrations. In the psalms, the canticle from The Book of Revelation and the Magnificat, the Church expresses her thanksgiving for redemption.

Christian tradition associates the newly-baptised with this evening office. The ceremony included a procession to the baptistry where, the evening before, these new Christians received the waters of re-birth. There they sang some psalms and the Magnificat as a grateful commemoration of the sacrament they had received. They also visited the chapel where they had been confirmed. This special Easter Vespers originated in Rome in the fifth or sixth century; from there it spread to other parts of Europe and has survived here and there down to our own times. It appealed so much to popular devotion that it was known as "the glorious office" (officium gloriosum).[8]

It was on this same evening, the first day of the week, that Jesus appeared to his disciples gathered together in the upper room in Jerusalem. The gospel recording this event is that of St John (20:19-31). It is read at Mass on the second Sunday of Easter, but on Easter Sunday the wonderful event which it recounts is commemorated in the Church's evening prayer. The Magnificat antiphon says: "On the evening of that Sunday, when the disciples were gathered behind locked doors, Jesus came and stood among them. He said to them, 'Peace be with you, alleluia'."

It is on this note of peace that Easter Sunday draws to an end. The celebration is not over, however: in an atmosphere of quiet and recollection it is continued at a more personal level. Together with the public and liturgical celebration there is "the intimate feast" of the heart.

Peace is Christ's special bequest to his disciples and to us on this day. Through his paschal mystery he has restored peace between God and man. He is himself our peace. And with this peace goes a great joy. With the disciples we can exclaim: "We have seen the Lord and are glad."

NOTES

1.   For this and other customs see K. Danaher, *The Year in Ireland*, The Mercier Press, Cork, 1972.
2.   The prayer following the seventh reading.
3.   D. Mollat, "La découverte du tombeau vide" in *Assemblées du Seigneur*, vol. 21, p. 100.
4.   *Assemblées du Seigneur* 21, p. 110.
5.   This gospel is also read on the third Sunday of Easter, Year A.

6. For example, versicle and response for prayer during the day (afternoon); Magnificat antiphon for evening prayer 1 of Sunday, week 3.

7. Throughout the year we have the prayer of vespers for Monday of the fourth week: "Stay with us, Lord Jesus, as evening falls; be our companion on our way. In your mercy inflame our hearts and raise our hope, so that, in union with our brethren, we may recognise you in the scriptures and in the breaking of bread."

8. J. Gaillard, *Holy Week and Easter,* The Liturgical Press, Collegeville, 1957, pp. 159-60.

Bibliography

General:
NOCENT, A., *The Liturgical Year,* Vol. 2, *Lent & Holy Week,* Liturgical Press, Collegeville, 1977.
The Liturgical Conference, Washington DC, *From Ashes to Easter,* revised ed. 1979.
HALMO, J., "Planning Lent, Triduum, Eastertime: A Survey of Pastoral Guidebooks" in *Worship* 56 (Jan. 1982), pp. 16-26.
REGAN, P., "The Three Days and the Forty Days" in *Worship* 54 (Jan. 1980), pp. 2-18.

Lent in the Eastern Church:
WILKINSON, J., *Egeria's Travels.* SPCK, London, 1978, pp. 132-40. Text and commentary.
MARY, M. & WARE, K., *The Lenten Triodion,* Faber, London and Boston, 1977.
A Monk of the Eastern Church, *The Year of Grace of the Lord,* Mowbray, London, 1980. See section on Lent and Holy Week.

The Lectionary in Lent:
Scripture in Church, a periodical published by Dominican Publications, Dublin (Irish and American editions). For commentary on Sunday (three-year cycle) and weekday readings see Nos. 1, 6, 10, 18, 22, 26, 30, 34, 38, 42. See also Biblical Essays: M. Maher, "The Lenten Lectionary" and J. McPolin, "Guide to the Liturgy of Weekdays of Lent" in No. 38 of this periodical, pp. 371-80 and 381-405.

Catechumenate and Baptism:
FIELD, A., *New Life* — What it meant to become a Christian in the early Church, Mowbray, London, 1978.

KAVANAGH, A., *The Shape of Baptism,* Pueblo, New York, 1978. Articles on the Christian Initiation of Adults by this author have appeared in *Worship* 48 (March 1974), pp. 143-52 and 53 (July 1979), pp. 341-56.

READY, W., (editor), *Becoming a Catholic Christian* — A Symposium on Christian Initiation, Sadlier, New York, 1979.

SEARLE, M., *Christening* — the Making of Christians, Mayhew, London, 1977.

Sacrament of Reconciliation:

Dublin Diocesan Liturgical Commission, *Celebrating the Sacrament of Penance* (a pamphlet), Veritas, Dublin, 1975.

QUINN, J., "Celebrating the Sacrament of Penance" in *The Furrow* (June 1976) pp. 339-51.

CRICHTON, J., *The Ministry of Reconciliation* — A Commentary on the Order of Penance, Chapman, London, 1974.

Collective, "Reconciliation" in *The Way* (October 1975); articles by W. Vogels, B. Ahern, C. Brusselmans and K. Donovan.

Collective, "The New Rites of Penance" in *Supplement to Doctrine and Life* 67 (1977).

Holy Week:

HOWELL, C., *Preparing for Easter* (revised edition), Chapman, London, 1972.

LOHR, A., *The Great Week* (unrevised), Longmans, London, 1958.

SWAYNE, S., "The Liturgy of Holy Week" in *Scripture in Church* 14, pp. 292-99.

HENDERSON, F., "The Chrism Mass of Holy Thursday" in *Worship* 51 (March 1977), pp. 149-58.

ZWARTKRUIS, T., "Chrism Mass, Bond of Unity" in *Notitiae* 152 (1979), pp. 187-88.

KICKHAM, E., "Washing of the Feet: Symbol and Example" in *Scripture in Church* 42 (1981), pp. 243-46.

BROWN, S., "The Good News Today: Reflections on the Passion-Paschal Lessons" in *Worship* 50 (March 1976), pp. 163-72.

BROWN, R., "The Passion According to John" in *Worship* 49 (March 1975), pp. 126-34.

REGAN, P., "Veneration of the Cross" in *Worship* 52 (Jan. 1978), pp. 2-12.

WINZEN, D., *The Great Sabbath Rest and the First Love,* Mt. Saviour Monastery, Pine City, New York, 1975. (A booklet).

RYAN, S., "The Easter Vigil: an Alternative Model" in *The Furrow* (May 1974), pp. 239-46; a summary in *Intercom* (Feb. 1975).

JONES, P., and Ó SEANACHÁIN, G., "The Easter Vigil" and "What to Say about Easter" in *Intercom* (March 1982).

Theology of Easter:

DURRWELL, F., *The Resurrection,* Sheed & Ward, London, 1960.

WANSBROUGH, H., *The Resurrection,* St Paul Publications, Slough, 1972.

LÉON-DUFOUR, X., *Resurrection and the Message of Easter,* Chapman, London, 1974.